The Three Pillars

The Three Pillars

How Family Politics Shaped the Earliest Church and the Gospel of Mark

BARBARA J. SIVERTSEN

WIPF & STOCK · Eugene, Oregon

THE THREE PILLARS
How Family Politics Shaped the Earliest Church and the Gospel of Mark

Copyright © 2010 Barbara J. Sivertsen. All rights reserved. Except for brief quotations in critical publications or reviews, no part of this book may be reproduced in any manner without prior written permission from the publisher. Write: Permissions, Wipf & Stock, 199 W. 8th Ave., Suite 3, Eugene, OR 97401.

Unless otherwise cited, all biblical quotations herein are taken from the New Revised Standard Version Bible, copyright © 1989, Division of Christian Education of the National Council of the Churches of Christ in the United States of America. Used by permission. All rights reserved.

Wipf & Stock
An Imprint of Wipf and Stock Publishers
199 W. 8th Ave., Suite 3
Eugene, OR 97401
www.wipfandstock.com

ISBN 13: 978-1-60899-603-2

Manufactured in the U.S.A.

Dedicated to
my children, Lauren and James,
and
my grandchildren, present and future

Contents

List of Figures • viii
List of Tables • viii
Abbreviations • ix
Introduction • xiii

PART I
1. The Brothers and Sisters of Jesus and the Family of Joseph • 1
2. The Genealogies of Jesus and the Family of Mary • 21
3. The Brothers and Sisters of Jesus and Their Role in the Early Church • 38

PART II
4. Peter and Mark in Rome • 51
5. The Composition of the Gospel of Mark • 66
6. Peter's Son and the Second Gospel • 76
7. Mark, the Disciples, and the Relatives of Jesus • 93

PART III
8. A Crucial Question and Its Answer • 101
9. The Beloved Disciple and the Fourth Gospel • 114
10. Concluding Remarks and Observations • 124

Bibliography • 129

Figures

Figure 1: Ancestors and Family of Joseph, Mary's Husband • 9
Figure 2: Ancestors and Family of Mary • 29
Figure 3: Map of Asia Minor in the Late First Century CE • 57
Figure 4: Map of Galilee and Adjacent Territories • 77
Figure 5: Sketch of Dining Positions at the Last Supper • 103
Figure 6: Map of Jerusalem at the Time of Jesus' Arrest • 105

Tables

Table 1: Naming of Sons in the Family of King Herod • 4
Table 2: Names of Goliath Family Sons • 5
Table 3: Jesus' Ancestors from Luke 3:23–31 • 6
Table 4: Principal End-Time Texts in Mark 13 Compared to the Caligula Crisis and Its Aftermath (39–44 CE) and the Jewish War (66–70 CE) • 72–73

Abbreviations

AB	Anchor Bible
ABD	*The Anchor Bible Dictionary.* 6 vols. Edited by David Noel Freedman. New York: Doubleday, 1992.
ABRL	Anchor Bible Reference Library
Ag. Ap.	Josephus, *Against Apion*
ANF	Ante-Nicene Fathers
Ann.	Tacitus, *Annales*
Ant.	Josephus, *Antiquities of the Jews*
APOT	*The Apocrypha and Pseudepigrapha of the Old Testament.* Edited by R. H. Charles. 2 vols. Oxford. 1913.
b.	Babylonian Talmud
BASOR	*Bulletin of the American Schools of Oriental Research*
BAR	*Biblical Archaeology Review*
BibInt	*Biblical Interpretation*
BTB	*Biblical Theology Bulletin*
CahRB	Cahiers de la Revue biblique
cf.	compare
CBQ	*Catholic Biblical Quarterly*
CD	Damascus Rule
Claud.	Suetonius, *Divus Claudius*
CQ	*Classical Quarterly*
Eccl. Hist.	Eusebius, *Ecclesiastical History*
EncJud	*Encyclopaedia Judaica.* 2d ed. 22 vols. Edited by Michael Berenbaum. Detroit and Jerusalem: Macmillan and Keter, 2007.
ErIsr	*Eretz-Israel*
FC	Fathers of the Church, Washington, D.C.

Gos. Mary	*Gospel of Mary*
Gos. Phil.	*Gospel of Philip*
Gos. Thom.	*Gospel of Thomas*
Haer.	Irenaeus, *Adversus haereses*. Against Heresies
HvTSt	*Hervormde teologiese studies*
IEJ	*Israel Exploration Journal*
ISBE	*International Standard Bible Encyclopedia*. Edited by G. W. Bromiley. 4 vols. Grand Rapids: Eerdmans, 1979–1988
JBL	*Journal of Biblical Literature*
JBQ	*Jewish Bible Quarterly*
JECS	*Journal of Early Christian Studies*
JETS	*Journal of the Evangelical Theological Society*
JNTS	*Journal of New Testament Studies*
JQR	*Jewish Quarterly Review*
JRASup	Journal of Roman Archaeology: Supplement Series
JSJ	*Journal for the Study of Judaism in the Persian, Hellenistic, and Roman Periods*
JSJSup	Journal for the Study of Judaism: Supplement Series
JSNT	*Journal for the Study of the New Testament*
JSNTSup	Journal for the Study of the New Testament: Supplement Series
JSPSup	Journal for the Study of the Pseudepigrapha: Supplement Series
JTS	*Journal of Theological Studies*
KJV	King James Version of the English Bible
LCL	Loeb Classical Library
Life	Josephus, *The Life*
m.	*Mishnah*
n., nn.	note, notes
NCB	New Century Bible
NHS	Nag Hammadi Studies
NovT	*Novum Testamentum*
NovTSup	Supplements to Novum Testamentum
NRSV	New Revised Standard Version of the English Bible
NTS	*New Testament Studies*
PNTC	Pelican New Testament Commentaries
Pan.	Epiphanius, *Panarion (Adversus haereses)*. Refutation of All Heresies

Prot. Jas.	*Protevangelium of James*
SBS	Stuttgarter Bibelstudien
SJLA	Studies in Judaism in Late Antiquity
SNTSMS	Society for New Testament Studies Monograph Series
SP	Sacra pagina
STAR	Studies in Theology and Religion, The Netherlands School for Advanced Studies in Theology and Religion
t.	*Tosefta*
TSAJ	Texte und Studien zum antiken Judentum
TU	*Texte und Untersuchungen*
War	Josephus, *Jewish War*
WUNT	Wissenschaftliche Untersuchungen zum Neuen Testament
y.	Jerusalem Talmud

Introduction

AFTER THE CRUCIFIXION OF Jesus of Nazareth in Jerusalem on 7 April, 30 CE[1] his followers, following an interval of hiding and a trip to Galilee,[2] gathered once more in Jerusalem and began to preach to the crowds who had come to the city for the Jewish festival of Shavuot or Pentecost.[3] Because of this, Pentecost is held by Christians to be the birthday or beginning of the Christian church.

It was not a church as we think of one, however, but rather a congregation, a gathering of believers, a religious movement that started in Jerusalem and spread throughout the Jewish homeland and eventually throughout the Mediterranean world. Our earliest information on the first decades of this movement comes from the New Testament book of Acts, from bits and pieces found in the surviving letters of the Apostle Paul,[4] and from a few brief and hotly contested mentions in the writings of early Jewish and pagan writers such as Josephus, Tacitus, and Suetonius.[5] This sparse information would be augmented in later centuries by writings of various church fathers and in the early fourth century by a church history by the Christian bishop Eusebius of Caesarea.

According to Eusebius, quoting second-century church father Clement of Alexandria, Jesus' principal disciples Peter, James, and John chose another James, referred to as James the Lord's brother or James the Just,

---

1. For this date see Finegan, *Handbook*, 295, 300–301; Meier, *Marginal Jew*, 402, 407. The terms BCE (Before Common Era) and CE (Common Era) will be used throughout this book. For the only other chronologically possible date, 3 April, 33 CE, see Humphrey and Waddington, "Astronomy," 165–81.
2. See Matt 28:16; Mark 16:7; John 20:19; 21:1–23.
3. Acts 2:14–41.
4. See, for example, Gal 1:13—2:14; 1 Cor 15:5–7.
5. Josephus, *Ant.* 18:63–64; Suetonius, *Claud.* 25:3–5; Tacitus, *Ann.* 15:44.

as the first bishop of Jerusalem.[6] Although the term bishop is anachronistic, the fact that James the Lord's brother was the leader of the early Christians is confirmed in the book of Acts and in the Apostle Paul's letter to the Galatians, in which Paul stated that the three reputed pillars of the church were James, Cephas (or Peter), and John.[7] Until his death by stoning at the hands of Jewish officials in Jerusalem in 62 CE,[8] James the Lord's brother led the early Christian church from Jerusalem while itinerant preachers, most notably the Apostle Paul but also including this James's brothers and the disciple Peter, spread the new faith through most of the Roman Empire.

Paul's three pillars—James the Lord's brother, Peter, and John—were of critical importance to the formation, direction, and maintaining of the movement that became the Christian church, and yet relatively little is actually known about them. Among modern writers, the Apostle Paul has attracted far more attention than any of these three pillars. Only in the last thirty years or so has there been a group of scholarly studies on James the Lord's brother,[9] climaxed by the popular uproar occasioned by the discovery of the James Ossuary in 2002.[10] On Peter, a recent popular work by Bart Ehrman[11] shows how little we actually know about this chief disciple of Jesus. The third pillar, John, is thought to be the son of Zebedee, one of Jesus' original twelve disciples, and the author of the Gospel of John, but this is far from certain. The identity of this John is linked to that of the beloved disciple in the Fourth Gospel. By one count, there have been twenty-four individuals proposed as the beloved disciple.[12]

In fact, surprisingly little personal information exists about any of the central figures of the earliest church. We do not know, for example, how many of Jesus' twelve principal disciples were married or the identi-

6. Eusebius, *Eccl. Hist.* 2:1:3.

7. Gal 2:9.

8. For James' death see Josephus, *Ant.* 20:197–203; Eusebius, *Eccl. Hist.* 2:23. For a discussion of this event and these sources, see Painter, *Just James*, 118–44.

9. See, for example, Bauckham, "James and the Jerusalem Church," 415–80; idem, "James and the Gentiles," 154–84; Bernheim, *James*; Chilton and Evans, *James the Just and Christian Origins*; Chilton and Neusner, *Brother of Jesus*; Painter, *Just James*. Robert H. Eisenman's *James the Brother of Jesus* puts forth the hypothesis that James was the Righteous Teacher of the Dead Sea Scrolls, an idea not accepted by most scholars.

10. Shanks and Witherington, *Brother of Jesus*.

11. Ehrman, *Peter, Paul, and Mary Magdalene*, 3–86.

12. Charlesworth, *Beloved Disciple*, 336–59.

ties of any of their wives. In the book of Acts, our principal source of information, neither James the Lord's brother nor Peter are referred to as being married. Only a chance mention in the Apostle Paul's first letter to the Corinthians and a story in the Gospel of Mark tells us that they were.[13] Nor do we know what role the disciples' families played in the emerging Christian community.

This lack of information on family relationships, usually noted only when scholars go searching for information on the role of women in the ministry of Jesus and in the earliest church,[14] is even more remarkable given the crucial role that kinship played in first-century Mediterranean society. Kinship was one of the two basic institutions in antiquity (the other being politics). As New Testament scholar K. C. Hanson writes, "virtually no social relationship, institution, or value set was untouched by the family and its concerns."[15] Kinship ties interacted with wealth, occupation, politics, and religion, and most importantly in ancient Mediterranean culture, ascribed honor was derived from one's family.[16] As I will show in this book, kinship played a key role in the conflict over leadership in the early church and between the church and Jerusalem's high-priestly hierarchy.

I have been a genealogist and family historian for most of my adult life, and as such I have long been aware of the information that can be obtained about a person from their genealogy, from the naming patterns within their families, and from the family traditions that have been passed down, altered and reinterpreted as these traditions usually are. When I was studying the two disparate genealogies of Jesus found in the New Testament Gospels of Matthew and Luke, I realized that there was much more information in these family trees than scholars had previously supposed. After sorting out the various sources behind these genealogies and using naming patterns—a staple source of information for genealogists—I was able to propose a model that accounted for the discrepancies between

13. 1 Cor 9:5; Mark 1:30–31.

14. See, for example, Schotroff, "Women as Followers of Jesus," 418–27; Witherington, *Women in the Ministry of Jesus*; D'Angelo, "Reconstructing 'Real' Women in Gospel Literature," 105–28. There is one notable historian for the family of Jesus, Richard Bauckham; see Bauckham, *Jude*; idem, "Salome the Sister of Jesus," 245–75; idem, "Mary of Clopas," 231–55.

15. Hanson, "All in the Family," 27.

16. Hanson, "BTB Readers Guide: Kinship," 183–94; Malina, *New Testament World*, 121–26. Barton, *Discipleship and Family Ties*, 36–37, notes how important marriage and kinship ties were for the first-century Jewish historian Josephus.

the two lineages and to suggest a reconstruction of the families of Mary and Joseph.[17] I did not, however, go into the implications of this work, particularly the significance of these families in the historical picture of Jesus' life. Only later did I realize the significance of family relationships in the leadership clashes among the early followers of Jesus. Only later again did I realize the critical role that another family relationship played in the survival of the earliest Christians in Jerusalem during the decades between Jesus' death and the Jewish revolt of 66–70 CE.

I eventually realized that certain family relationships involving the three pillars—James, Peter, and John—played a crucial role in the leadership, doctrine, and survival of the earliest Christian movement and profoundly affected the writing of the earliest Gospel, the Gospel of Mark. More important, I realized that the family rivalry I had discovered answered questions about this Gospel that have puzzled scholars and laymen for centuries. For example, why is the writer of Mark so hostile to both the family of Jesus and the twelve disciples, especially Peter? Why does he write in "sandwiches" and include repetitive episodes, such as the feeding of the four or five thousand? Why is there no birth story or genealogy in Mark? Where did Mark's story of the Passion come from? Who is the naked young man in the garden of Gethsemane on the night Jesus was arrested? And most important, why does the Gospel of Mark end so abruptly, with the statement that the women at the tomb said nothing, out of fear, about what they have seen?

In the following chapters I will explore first, the family of James and the role this kin group played in James's appointment to head the early followers of Jesus. Second, I will discuss the family of Peter and the writing of the book of Mark. Third, I will show that the final pillar, John, was indeed the beloved disciple but someone entirely different from the son of Zebedee. Because of his family, this John was crucial to the survival of the Christian movement in Jerusalem.

---

17. Sivertsen, "New Testament Genealogies," 43–50.

The Brothers and Sisters of Jesus and the Family of Joseph

THE BROTHERS AND SISTERS OF JESUS

IN THE GOSPEL OF Mark four individuals are named as the brothers of Jesus: James, Joses, Judas and Simon. In the Gospel of Matthew they are called James, Joseph, Simon and Judas. The texts also mention unnamed sisters. Given the virtually universal custom of naming siblings in birth order, James was the oldest of the brothers followed by Joseph, and either Judas (Jude) and Simon or Simon and Judas. The Apostle Paul also refers to James the brother of the Lord in his letter to the Galatians and to the Lord's brothers in his first letter to the Corinthians.[1]

What exactly do the terms "brothers" and "sisters" mean here? In Greek the word for brother is *adelphos*. In the second century a Palestinian Jewish Christian named Hegesippus wrote about the family of Jesus. His writings, quoted in Eusebius's *History of the Church*, indicate that the brothers of Jesus were in fact sons of Joseph in the usual way.[2] Other second-century writers, and a legendary mid-second-century account of the births of Mary and Jesus entitled the *Protevangelium of James*,[3] treat these brothers as stepbrothers of Jesus, sons of Joseph by an earlier wife. This point of view has become known as the Epiphanian view, after a fourth-century writer who espoused it.[4]

According to Epiphanius, Joseph Mary's husband is supposed to have had his oldest son James when he was aged forty and to have been over eighty when he wed Mary.[5] That would mean that James would have

---

1. Gal 1:19 and 1 Cor 9:5.

2. Eusebius, *Eccl. Hist.* 3:11; 4:22:4. Hegesippus calls Simeon a cousin of the Lord and the son of James's uncle Clopas who was a brother of Joseph's.

3. Cullmann and Higgins, "Protevangelium," 374–88.

4. See Epiphanius, *Panarion of St. Epiphanius*, 90–91, 229, 348–51.

5. Epiphanius, *Pan.* 78:8:1–2.

been over forty himself at the time of Jesus' birth. Since both the Gospels of Matthew and Luke put Jesus' birth in the reign of King Herod, who died before the Passover in 4 BCE,[6] James would have been *at least* 106 years old at his death in 62 CE!

This is wildly unrealistic. Generally, even wealthy Jewish men did not survive beyond their sixties in the first century,[7] while the first-century emperors Augustus and Tiberius who lived into their seventies where considered highly unusual survivals.

The *Protevangelium of James*, which I believe does contain a few earlier and genuine oral traditions about Jesus' family, is nevertheless a legendary work. As oral historians have long known, stories are recombined and reinterpreted as the needs of the group telling the story change through time.[8] The *Protevangelium* is in fact most concerned with suggesting the perpetual virginity of Mary the mother of Jesus. This is why it makes Joseph an old man. It also includes a story in which the midwife's assistant, named Salome, puts her finger out to feel for Mary's virginity only to have the finger burned, then miraculously healed by the newborn Jesus.

The *Protevangelium of James* is a rough contemporary of another legendary Christian account, *The Acts of Paul and Thecla*, in which the heroine, Thecla, hears the Apostle Paul preach thus: "Blessed are the bodies of the virgins, for these will be pleasing to God and will not lose the reward for their chastity."[9] Thereafter in the story, Thecla maintains her virginity only through a series of miraculous rescues. This emphasis on virginity and chastity was first stressed by Paul in an apocalyptic context in the mid-first century because Paul believed the return of Jesus was imminent and people should prepare for it by living chastely. By the second century chastity had developed into a lifestyle ideal to prepare Christians for eternal life in heaven.[10] This time period was when the idea of the perpetual virginity of Mary became so important to Gentile Christians, who by then made up the majority in the church. The idea of Mary's perpetual virginity had no connection to first-century Judaism, where the ideal for men was to be fruitful and multiply and for their wives to be

---

6. Hoehner, "Date of the Death of Herod," 101–11.

7. Crossan and Reed, *Excavating Jesus*, 20, point out that life expectancy for those who survived childhood was in the thirties and that "those reaching fifty or sixty were rare."

8. Vansina, *Oral Tradition*, 118–22; see also Sivertsen, *Parting of the Sea*, 49–50 for an example.

9. Ehrman, *Peter, Paul, and Mary Magdalene*, 147.

10. Ibid., 149.

the biological conduits of this command. According to Jewish Mishnaic law (compiled about 200 CE but referring to situations earlier in time), if the wife refused to have intercourse with her husband, he was required to divorce her.[11] Mary and Joseph, as married first-century Jews, would have thought it a matter of righteousness to have produced children, and a matter of disobedience to God to abstain from procreation.

In the late fourth century, another view of the brothers of Jesus was articulated by the church father Jerome who wrote a tract *Against Helvidius* (Helvidius held the view that the brothers and sisters were children of Mary and Joseph). In defending Mary's status as a perpetual virgin (and Joseph's status as a celibate), Jerome wrote that the biblical term "brothers" meant in fact "cousins" and that James and Joses identified as the sons of Mary in Mark 15:40 were the sons of Joseph's brother Clopas.[12] Jerome did not really account for the other two sons, Judas and Simon, but by inference they were cousins as well. Modern scholarship has in general rejected this view, in part because there is a very clear Greek term for cousin, *anepsios*, which is not used in the Bible to describe James, Joses, Judas or Simon.[13] In fact, some biblical scholars such as Giza Vermes have suggested that Jesus was actually a child of Joseph and Mary.[14]

FIRST-CENTURY JEWISH NAMING PATTERNS

My own research on Jewish naming patterns in first-century Palestine strongly suggests that Jesus was not the son of Joseph, however. Looking at the naming patterns for sons in two first-century Palestinian Jewish families for which sufficient information is available, King Herod's family and the Goliath family of Jericho (see tables 1 and 2), I discovered that the predominant pattern was to name a firstborn son for his father or his father's father.[15] This pattern is also found in the first part of the Jewish royal Hasmonean dynasty (167–37 BCE), in which Mattathias son of John son of Simon named his oldest son John and his next son Simon.[16] According to

---

11. *m. Nedarim* 11:12; see discussion in Wegner, *Chattel or Person?*, 41, 58–60, 78–83.

12. For a fuller description of this view and its modern variants see Bauckham, *Jude*, 20–23.

13. Bauckham, *Jude*, 23–24; Meier, "Brothers and Sisters of Jesus," 19–21; Shanks and Witherington, *Brother of Jesus*, 202–4.

14. Vermes, *Changing Faces of Jesus*, 163–64.

15. Sivertsen, "New Testament Genealogies," 45–46.

16. 1 Macc 2:1–3.

4 THE THREE PILLARS

biblical researcher Tal Ilan, *paponymy*, the naming of a son for the grandfather, was one of the most common naming procedures for Palestinian Jews of this time, which is often referred to as the late Second Temple period, with the entire Second Temple period extending from 538 BCE to 70 CE.[17] Only secondarily were other names in the father's lineage used for firstborn sons, although such names were favored for younger sons.[18]

TABLE 1. Naming of Sons in the Family of King Herod

	Son named for father	Son named for father's father	Son named for father's paternal grandfather	Son named for mother's father	Son named for father's brother	Son named for mother's brother	Son named for other father's kin	Son named for other mother's kin	Other
First known son	6	5	1	2	1		1		3
Second son		1*		1 / 1*		1		1†	4
Younger sons	6	1		1	1			2	3

NOTE: Data from Hanson, "Herodians and Mediterranean Kinship. Part I," 78–81. Uncertain relationships (denoted by a question mark therein) are not included. Nineteen (45 percent) of the sons were named for the father or the father's father. Twenty-three (55 percent) were named for the father's family; nine (21 percent) for the mother's family.

* Son named for both father's and mother's kin.
† Named for the mother.

17. Ilan, *Lexicon*, 32.
18. Hachlili, "Names and Nicknames," 9–10, 192–93; idem, "Hebrew Names, Personal Names," 88–89.

TABLE 2. Names of Goliath Family Sons

Named for the father	Named for the father's father	Named for the father's brother	Other
Yehoezer #26 Yehoezer #28* Yehoezer Akabia #23* Yehoezer Akabia #31*	Eleazar #6 Yehoezer #19 Yehoezer #3 Yehoezer #4 Yehoezer #5	Ishmael #28	Ishmael #17 Natanel #12 Simon #21 Menahem #20

NOTE: Positive and probable identifications are included; possible relationships are not. Data taken from Hachlili, "Goliath Family," 66.

*Also named for the father's father.

This practice of naming a firstborn son for the father is found in the family of John the Baptist, where the name Zechariah is first proposed for the infant son of Zechariah and Elizabeth. When Elizabeth says the baby is to be called John the people say *to her* that none of her relatives has this name.[19] This story confirms that Elizabeth is a relative of her husband's, probably through the male line. As scholars have pointed out, marriage between close relatives was a common practice in first-century Israel, and priestly families such as that of Zechariah and Elizabeth practiced so much intermarriage that many physical defects that rendered priests unfit for temple service were genetic in nature and possibly the result of inbreeding.[20]

COMPARISON OF THE GENEALOGIES OF JESUS

Does this naming pattern apply to James and his brothers? Let's compare the names of the four brothers to the names in the two genealogies of Jesus found in Matt 1:2–16 and Luke 3:23–38. Both genealogies claim to trace Jesus' ancestry through his supposed father, Joseph. The two genealogies express different theological themes, most clearly shown in the inclusion of four women of somewhat dubious reputation in the earlier part of Matthew's list and the tracing of the male line back to Adam, "the son of God," in Luke's.[21] The list in Matthew starts from Abraham and works forward, while Luke's list starts with Jesus and works backward. Both lists

---

19. Luke 1:59–61.

20. Hanson, "Herodians and Mediterranean Kinship. Part II," 143; Jeremias, *Jerusalem*, 365–66; Johnson, *Genealogies*, 97.

21. Brown, *Birth*, 66–85.

trace Joseph's descent from King David through Zerubbabel, the sixth-century BCE post-exilic (the exile occurred from 586 to 538 BCE) leader of Judea. However, while Matthew follows the Judean king lists found in the Old Testament (although he leaves out four kings), Luke uses a long list of unknown names to connect King David to Zerubbabel through a younger son of David's, Nathan (see table 3). Even more peculiar, Joseph's father is called Jacob in Matthew's genealogy but Heli (Eli) in Luke's.

TABLE 3. Jesus' Ancestors from Luke 3:23–31

43. *David*	22. *Shealtiel*	18. Joda (Judah?)
42. *Nathan*	21. *Zerubbabel*	17. Josech (Joseph?)
41. Mattatha	20. Rhesa	16. Semein (Simeon?)
40. Menna	19. *Joanan*	15. Mattathias
39. Melea		14. Maath
38. Eliakim		13. Naggai
37. Jonam		12. Esli
36. Joseph		11. Nahum
35. Judah		10. Amos
34. Simeon		9. Mattathias
33. Levi		8. Joseph
32. Matthat		7. Jannai
31. Jorim		6. Melchi
30. Eliezer		5. Levi
29. Joshua		**4. Matthat**
28. Er		3. Heli
27. Elmadam		2. *Joseph*
26. Cosam		1. *Jesus*
25. Addi		
24. Melchi		
23. Neri		

Note: historically attested names in italics; related blocks of names (see text) in bold.

These differences are not typical of the inconsistencies found in most traditional genealogies.[22] Leaving aside the standard biblical genealogies of the ancestors of King David, I believe the differences in the more recent sections of the genealogies in Matthew and Luke are the result of four *different and independent genealogical sources, incorrectly combined*. These four sources are

1) the name of Joseph's father in Matthew
2) the name of Joseph's father in Luke

22. Wilson, *Genealogy and History*, 46–54; Vansina, *Oral Tradition*, 101, 182–83.

3) the names from Zerubbabel to Joseph's father in Matthew
4) the names from David to Zerubbabel and from Zerubbabel to Joseph's father in Luke.[23]

It is important to recognize that the sources for the name of Joseph's father are independent from the rest of these two lineages. Modern genealogists have long recognized this phenomenon, since the names of one's father and grandfathers are usually a matter of personal experience and memory, while the names of earlier generations of ancestors are most often passed on secondhand, either orally or through written records.[24]

Which then, of the two names for Joseph's father given in the New Testament genealogies is more likely to be the correct one? Following the most common naming pattern for first-century Jews, Joseph probably named his oldest son for his father. Presuming that James was Joseph's oldest son, Joseph's father was thus Jacob, the Semitic form of James, as it is in the genealogy of Matthew.[25] This traditional name for Joseph's father was probably part of what scholars call the M tradition, which was carried to the city of Antioch in Syria by refugees from the Jerusalem Christian community after the fall of Jerusalem to the Romans in 70 CE. Later it was incorporated into Matthew's Gospel.[26] How it got connected to the most recent names in Matthew's genealogy will be discussed in the next chapter. For the present, however, we can see that the names of Joseph's younger sons—Joses or Joseph, Judah, and Simon or Simeon—are not found in Matthew's genealogical list, but in Luke's!

LUKE'S GENEALOGY FROM DAVID TO JOSEPH

The genealogy in Luke contains seventy-seven names from Adam to Jesus. It has been suggested that this number has some ritual significance and that this list was passed down by the relatives of Jesus to the writer of Luke's Gospel.[27] There are forty-one names from King David's son Nathan to Jesus, too many to occupy the pre- and post-exilic periods of Israelite history (see table 3). This overabundance of names is a form of embellishment,

---

23. Sivertsen, "New Testament Genealogies," 44.

24. Jacobus, "Nature of Genealogical Evidence," 213–20; idem, "Confessions," 82, 84, 85.

25. Sivertsen, "New Testament Genealogies," 44, 46.

26. See Painter's summary of B. H. Streeter's hypothesis in Painter, *Just James*, 86–88.

27. Bauckham, *Jude*, 316–26, 355–60.

8   THE THREE PILLARS

a phenomenon often found in traditional genealogies. Also, many of the names in the supposedly pre-exilic (before 586 BCE) segment, those between Nathan and Shealtiel, are the names of patriarchs, which are almost never found before the exile but are common in the post-exilic period, especially in Second Temple times.[28] This is a form of anachronism.

The only historically attested names on Luke's list among these forty-one after King David's son Nathan are Zerubbabel and his father Shealtiel and Joanan, the son of Rhesa, son of Zerubbabel. Joanan is Hananiah, the son of Zerubbabel in 1 Chr 3:19, 21. The name Rhesa actually means "head" in Aramaic and is a title for Zerubbabel.[29] That a title has become a name in Luke's genealogy suggests that the original genealogy was a simple list of names written in Aramaic, not linked by "son" or "begat," and that whoever translated this list into Greek was unaware of this word's meaning.[30] That the name Rhesa appears as a son of Zerubbabel indicates that in its present form the list is in reverse order.

Most importantly, within these forty-one entries in Luke's list there are three blocks of names that range from very similar to near-identical and occur in the same or nearly the same order. Counting up from Jesus (number one), these blocks occur

1) at numbers four to eight: Matthat, Levi, Melchi, Jannai, Joseph
2) at numbers fifteen to eighteen: Mattathias, Semein (Simeon?), Josech (Joseph?), and Joda (Judah?); and
3) at numbers thirty-two to thirty-six: Matthat, Levi, Simeon, Judah, and Joseph (see table 3). The repeated occurrence of some version of the name Mattathias serves to set off each of these blocks.

The peculiar characteristics in Luke's genealogical list are very similar to features in the pre-Roman king list found in Geoffrey of Monmouth's eleventh-century CE *History of the Kings of Britain*. Archaeologist Stuart Piggott discovered that Geoffrey's list contained far more names than was necessary (embellishment), that the oldest names were in fact from some of the more recent (sixth-century CE and later) Welsh ruling families (anachronism), that repetitions of blocks of identical names occurred

---

28. Jeremias, *Jerusalem*, 296, 330–31; Johnson, *Genealogies*, 229–30.
29. Jeremias, *Jerusalem*, 296; Bauckham, *Jude*, 333.
30. Bauckham, *Jude*, 328–29.

The Brothers and Sisters of Jesus and the Family of Joseph 9

at irregular intervals throughout one section, and that certain names divided large groups of names on the list.[31]

The cause for such similar genealogical features in Luke's post-David genealogy and in the ancient British king list is probably the same: genealogies of various lengths were combined to make an attractively long single genealogy. The three repeated blocks in the Lukan genealogy are either variant pedigrees of a family line combined sequentially or collateral lines of a family converted into direct ancestors. Because these blocks, or family lines, were combined with the other names, the overlong length of the list caused someone to scrap the conventional ancestors of Zerubbabel—that is, the Judean kings—and instead insert some of the list's names in their place.

Because the forty-one most recent names in Luke's genealogy are evidently reversed, the block with numbers thirty-two to thirty-six—Matthat, Levi, Simeon, Judah, and Joseph—would in fact be the most recent real family line, in reverse order, with Joseph the most recent name and Matthat (a form of Matthew) the oldest. Having Joseph, the most recent name, as the father of Jacob and grandfather of Joseph follows the Second Temple naming practice of *paponymy* mentioned above—that Joseph Mary's husband was named after his grandfather (see figure 1).

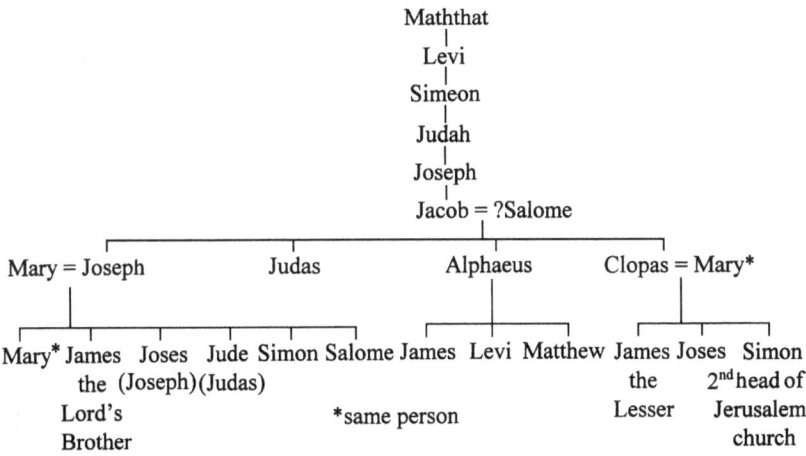

FIGURE 1. Ancestors and family of Joseph, Mary's husband.

---

31. Piggott, "Sources of Geoffrey of Monmouth," 269–86.

When it came to naming his own sons, Joseph Mary's husband named his oldest son after his own father, and then named his younger sons after his grandfather Joseph (or Joses), his great-grandfather Judah or Judas, and his great-great-grandfather Simeon or Simon. This naming pattern follows the practice of naming younger sons for members of the father's lineage. Jacob, Joseph's father, was himself probably a younger son, named for some significant person in his mother's lineage. This was also a naming practice in Second Temple times.[32]

While the names of Jesus' four brothers clearly fit comfortably within the lineage of Joseph as shown in figure 1, the name Jesus does not. The only Jesus (i.e., Joshua) found in Luke's genealogy is in Luke 3:29: Joshua son of Eliezer, which does not appear to have anything to do with the recent ancestors in Joseph's family. In fact, had Jesus been the firstborn son of Joseph he would have been named for Joseph's father Jacob. Had Jesus been a younger son (after the four brothers), he probably would have been named Matthew or Levi, the other names in this lineage. As we will see in the next chapter, Jesus was not named for the most recent men in Mary's family either.

THE DAUGHTERS OF JOSEPH

The earliest and best attested names for Joseph's daughters are Mary (Semitic: Miriam; Greek: Mariamme or Mariamne) and Salome.[33] These were the two most popular Jewish women's names in Palestine in late Second Temple times, together constituting 48 percent of the named female population.[34] The name of Mary for Jesus' sister is also attested to in the third-century *Gospel of Philip*.[35]

Although there is far less evidence for naming practices for Jewish women in Second Temple times than for men, what does exist suggests that women were often named for their grandmothers.[36] I think this is the case in Joseph's family. When items in a traditional story do not make

---

32. Hanson, "Herodians and Mediterranean Kinship. Part I," 82; table 1, this volume.

33. Epiphanius *Pan.* 78:8:1; 78:9:6; see Bauckham, "Salome the Sister of Jesus," 246 n. 4.

34. Ilan, *Lexicon*, 9.

35. Isenberg, "Gospel of Philip," 135–36; see also Bauckham, "Salome the Sister of Jesus," 247.

36. Ilan, *Lexicon*, 32.

sense, they are likely to be from an earlier account or even the original source.[37] Therefore, the Salome who inexplicably appears as the midwife's assistant in the *Protevangelium of James* may in fact have been part of an early story in which Joseph's mother witnessed an examination of Mary, Joseph's betrothed, to see if Mary was indeed pregnant. It would be logical to have such an examination, since the honor of Joseph's family was at stake, and also to have a representative of Joseph's family (female of course) present, particularly since Jewish custom called for at least two witnesses when evidence needed to be assured.[38] Later this story migrated, as stories do in oral traditions, to the more notable event, the birth of Jesus. Then in the second century it became transformed into a miracle story proving the perpetual virginity of Mary (see above). Looking back to the original story, I believe this provides an indication that Jesus' sister Salome was named for her paternal grandmother.

In the New Testament, the name Salome appears only at the end of the Gospel of Mark along with Mary the mother of James the lesser and Joses, and Mary Magdalene. These three women witness Jesus' burial and on the third day go to Jesus' tomb.[39] Since it was the Jewish practice for the closest relatives of the deceased to perform the duties at burial and later, on the third day after burial, at the tomb,[40] we should presume that both Mary the mother of James the lesser and Joses and Salome were in fact Jesus' sisters. Mary Magdalene's place in this kin group remains obscure, but since in John 20:16 she calls the risen Jesus "teacher" she was not a member of his family.

THE BROTHERS OF JOSEPH

According to Eusebius, Joseph had a brother, Clopas, the father of the Simon or Simeon who succeeded James the Lord's brother as head of the Jerusalem church; this is almost certainly the same Clopas mentioned in John 19:25 and the Cleopas found in Luke 24:18.[41] Clopas is *not* the same name as Alphaeus (*Ḥalphai*), mentioned in the Gospel of Mark and

---

37. Vansina, *Oral Tradition*, 93; Sivertsen, *Parting of the Sea*, 153.
38. Bauckham, *Eyewitnesses*, 49, citing Gerhardsson, "Mark and the Female Witnesses," 218.
39. Mark 15:40; 16:1.
40. Hachlili, *Jewish Funerary Customs*, 479–83.
41. Eusebius, *Eccl. Hist.* 3:11; 4:22; Bauckham, *Eyewitnesses*, 87 n. 79.

in Acts—the names Alphaeus and Clopas have different Semitic roots.[42] According to an early Christian writer Anastasius of Sinai, Clopas was married to Mary, the daughter of Joseph (see Mary of Clopas in John 19:25).[43] It was not uncommon for a Jewish woman to marry her father's brother in this period.[44] It kept the dowry payment within the family and may have offered some protection to the wife from abuse and divorce.

Other later Christian writers also identified the wife of Clopas as the mother of James the lesser and Joses.[45] This would mean that Clopas had sons James the lesser, Joses, and Simon, and that in terms of naming patterns he named his oldest son James for his father Jacob (James in Greek), his next son Joses (or Joseph) for his grandfather, and his youngest son Simon (Semitic: Simeon), either for his great-great grandfather (probably with an intervening son, Judas, having died young) or for himself. If his formal name were Simon, Clopas would have been a nickname to distinguish him from all the other Simons since Simon or Simeon was the most common Jewish male name of the time.[46] The naming pattern for Clopas's sons is thus the same naming pattern found in the family of Joseph.

Listed elsewhere among Jesus' disciples were James son of Alphaeus and Levi son of Alphaeus.[47] The name Alphaeus is Aramaic and means "God has replaced [*sc.* a dead child]"[48] and was likely another nickname. In Matt 9:9 the name of Levi son of Alphaeus was replaced by the name Matthew, but the occupation as tax collector was retained. The early third-century Christian writer Julius Africanus wrote that he received a tradition from Hebrew genealogists that Eli (the name of Joseph's father in the Gospel of Luke), Matthat, and Levi were brothers, sons of Melchi (number six in Luke's genealogy).[49] This statement likely reflects an earlier tradition, that Levi son of Alphaeus and the Matthew found in the First Gospel were indeed brothers, although not of Eli and not sons of Melchi—this was an attempt by Christians at a much later time to integrate the original tradition of Matthew and Levi being brothers into Luke's

---

42. Bauckham, *Jude*, 17.
43. Anastasius, *Quaestio* 153; see Blinzler, *Brüder und Schwestern Jesu*, 36.
44. Vermes, *Complete Dead Sea Scrolls*, 69–70; Jerimias, *Jerusalem*, 218, 365–66.
45. Blinzler, *Brüder und Schwestern Jesu*, 36.
46. Ilan, *Lexicon*, 56.
47. Matt 10:3; Mark 2:14; 3:18; Luke 6:15; Acts 1:13.
48. Williams, "Palestinian Jewish Personal Names," 94.
49. Wallraff, *Julius Africanus Chronographiae*, 273.

The Brothers and Sisters of Jesus and the Family of Joseph 13

genealogy, which had a Matthew and a Levi. Jacob or James, Levi, and Matthew are all names in Joseph's family and lineage; therefore I think it likely that Alphaeus was another brother of Joseph's, probably older than Clopas and younger than Joseph (see figure 1).

Another of Jesus' disciples was Judas [son] of James. The name James (that is, Jacob) was far more common among members of the early Christian community in Palestine than it was among Palestinian first-century Jewish men as a whole, being the third most common (tied with Judas) in the Gospels and Acts and only eleventh among Palestinian male Jews.[50] Because of the prevalence of the name Jacob or James in the family of Joseph, I think that Jesus' disciple Jude or Judas the son of James was another, younger, brother of Joseph's.

This would mean that the disciples Levi, Matthew, James son of Alphaeus and Judas son of James would all have been kinsmen of Jesus through his ostensible father Joseph. Given how important kinship ties were, and the ascribed honor they represented in the society of Jesus' time, the presence of these relatives around Jesus as his disciples would have lent legitimacy to his ministry, especially since his own brothers were not his followers in his lifetime.[51]

HISTORICAL MEANING OF THE NAMES IN JOSEPH'S FAMILY

Through Zerubbabel, a descendant of the Judean kings, Joseph's family claimed descent from David. However, the family names of Joseph's most recent ancestors (see figure 1) are taken from the royal Hasmonean dynasty, not from the earlier Judean kings.

In the first part of the second century BCE, Israel was ruled by Hellenistic Greek-speaking kings known as Seleucids, whose capital was in Syria. In 175 BCE the Seleucid ruler Antiochus IV Epiphanes raided the Jerusalem temple.[52] In 169 BCE his forces took over Jerusalem, causing the flight of many of its inhabitants and the start of resistence to the Hellenizing segment of the city's population.[53] Two years later Antiochus IV initiated pagan sacrifices in the temple and sent agents to the surround-

---

50. Bauckham, *Eyewitnesses*, 85 (table 6), 90 (table 8).

51. For Jesus' brothers see Mark 3:31–35; John 7:5–8.

52. 1 Macc 1:20–24; 2 Macc 5:11–16. For the dates see Harrington, *Maccabean Revolt*, 88–89.

53. 1 Macc 1:29–53; 2 Macc 5:24–26, 6:1–11.

ing towns to enforce worship of the Greek gods. In the town of Modein, eighteen miles northwest of Jerusalem, these agents encountered a priest named Mattathias. Because of their ancestor Asmoneus, Mattathias and his descendants became known as Hasmoneans. Mattathias and his sons started a rebellion against Seleucid rule that eventually led to an independent Jewish state under one of Mattathias's sons, Simon (142–35 BCE). Simon made himself high priest and ruler and was followed by his son John Hyrcanus I (135–4 BCE) and John's sons Aristobulus I (104–3 BCE) and Alexander Jannaeus (103–76 BCE).[54]

Hasmonean family names became wildly popular in Israel from the earlier second century BCE through the mid-first century BCE. According to Tal Ilan, 31.5 percent of the Jewish male population in Palestine bore the names of the priest Mattathias and his five sons: John, Simon, Judah, Eleazar, and Jonathan. Adding the name of a sixth son mentioned in 2 Macc 8:22, Joseph, the percentage goes up to 39.9 percent.[55] These were, in effect, nationalistic names, as were the names of two important women in the dynasty, Salome and Mariamme.[56]

The Hasmonean names in Joseph's ancestry indicate that Joseph's ancestors were Hasmonean supporters from the very beginning of the Jewish revolt, at a time when Mattathias and his sons were holed up in the Judean hills, strengthening their contacts with villagers in the Judean countryside, and forming a people's militia under Mattathias's son, Judah the Maccabee. Looking back at the ancestors of Joseph (numbers thirty-two to thirty-six in the Lukan genealogy; see table 3 and figure 1) one sees this line begins with Matthat, a version of the same name as the hero priest who started the revolt: Mattathias. Estimating the birth of Joseph Mary's husband at about 25 BCE and counting back the generations in Joseph's family, allowing twenty-three to twenty-four years per generation,[57] places the birth of Matthat at about 163–69 BCE, in the beginning years of the revolt in Judea.

---

54. Coogan, "Chronolological Table of Rulers," 533ES.
55. Ilan, *Lexicon*, 6–7.
56. Sawicki, "Magdalenes and Tiberiennes," 185–86.
57. According to the Mishnah (*m. 'Abot* 5.21) the age for marriage of Israelite males was eighteen. In at least one traditional society, that of Hawaiian chieftains, the generation length was twenty to twenty-five years (Masse et al., "Waha'ula *heiau*," 19–56). In light of these two items, the estimated generation length suggested here is not unreasonable.

The Brothers and Sisters of Jesus and the Family of Joseph 15

The fact that Joseph's family claimed descent from King David suggests that the family's origin was in Judea, as does their early support for the Hasmoneans. So how did they get to Nazareth, in Galilee, where Luke 2:4 says Joseph came from? Galilee only came under Hasmonean rule after 104 BCE, although the Hasmonean king Alexander Jannaeus was brought up in Galilee.[58] Another name in the Lukan genealogy, Jannai (number six back from Jesus), may be related to the name of this first Hasmonean ruler of Galilee. If this Jannai were actually part of a cognate line to Joseph's, counting back the generations would give an estimated birth date of Jannai at about 98–96 BCE, early in Alexander Jannaeus's reign.

Scholars have pointed out that after Galilee came under Hasmonean rule, Judean officials and their families moved to a series of fortified administrative centers there, including Sepphoris, where many functioned as tax collectors.[59] Later, under the rule of King Herod and into the first century CE, the descendants of these Hasmonean officials in Galilee remained clustered around the former administrative centers, keeping up their ties to the south through intermarriage, and returning to Jerusalem for the religious festivals.[60] According to the Gospels, Joseph and his family lived close to the administrative center of Sepphoris, kept up ties with Bethlehem in the south, and celebrated the festivals of Passover and Tabernacles in Jerusalem. Thus I believe the ancestors of Joseph were retainers of the Hasmoneans who moved to Galilee in the early first century BCE.

JOSEPH'S FAMILY: PEASANTS OR RETAINERS?

In the first century CE, the retainer class constituted about 5 percent of the population. They were the tax gatherers, police, scribes, and priests. Below the retainers were merchants, artisans, peasant farmers and fishermen. Below even these were the beggars, criminals, prostitutes and cripples.[61]

Jesus has often been described as a Mediterranean peasant rather than a member of the retainer class,[62] and by inference Joseph's family

---

58. Freyne, *Galilee*, 25; Josephus, *Ant.* 13:322.
59. Horsley, *Galilee: History, Politics, People*, 143; Freyne, *Galilee*, 27.
60. Sawicki, "Magdalenes and Tiberiennes," 187–88.
61. Rohrbaugh, *New Testament in Cross-Cultural Perspective*, 22–24.
62. See, most notably, Crossan, *Historical Jesus*; see also Oakman, "Was Jesus a Peasant?," 123–40.

would have been peasants as well. The most direct evidence for this designation is the statement about Jesus in Mark 6:3: "Is not this the carpenter?" In Matt 13:55 this is modified to: "Is not this the carpenter's son?" New Testament scholar John Dominic Crossan notes that the peasant artisan, such as he presumes Jesus to be, would be even lower than a rural peasant farmer in the social hierarchy of first-century Palestine, following anthropologist Gerhard Lenski's model that artisans were originally dispossessed peasants and their non-inheriting sons.[63]

In both Mark and Matthew the original Greek word for carpenter is *tektōn*. *Tektōn* does not necessarily mean carpenter, however. In fact, it was most often used as a generalized word for a craftsman or a builder in wood, stone, or metal. After an exhaustive look at the word *tektōn* in classical, biblical, and extra-biblical texts, and the references to wood, stone, and building in the Gospel sayings of Jesus, K. M. Campbell concluded that the usage "builder" would be a more accurate description of the term as it applied to Jesus and his father, and that Jesus' own sayings clearly show more of an affinity to construction than to any other activity.[64] Moreover, Campbell also found that the allusions in Jesus' teaching to construction and finance together were more numerous and significant than his allusions to agriculture, suggesting that Jesus and Joseph ran a family construction business.[65]

According to the Jewish historian Josephus, after the death of King Herod, revolts sprang up in Judea, Jericho, and Galilee. In putting down the revolt in Galilee, the town of Sepphoris was destroyed by an army under the Roman legate Varus, and the people of Sepphoris were sold into slavery.[66] Herod's son, Herod Antipas, inherited Galilee and spent the first years of his reign rebuilding Sepphoris. It has been speculated that Joseph and his sons worked at Sepphoris as a part of this rebuilding effort.[67] Rather than being peasant artisans, many of the builders in Sepphoris would have been highly skilled and well-paid workers. This is also suggested in the *Protevangelium of James*, in which Joseph is a builder.[68]

63. Crossan, *Birth of Christianity*, 155.
64. Campbell, "Occupation," 501–19.
65. Ibid., 518.
66. Josephus, *War* 2:68; *Ant*. 17:289.
67. Batey, "Carpenter," 249–58.
68. *Prot. Jas.* 9:1; 13:1; see Cullmann and Higgins, "Protevangelium," 379, 381.

The other biblical passage that implies the poverty of Joseph is Luke 2:22–24, which says "When the time came for their purification according to the law of Moses, they brought him [Jesus] up to Jerusalem to present him to the Lord (as it is written in the law of the Lord, 'Every firstborn male shall be designated as holy to the Lord'), and they offered a sacrifice according to what is stated in the law of the Lord, 'a pair of turtledoves, or two young pigeons.'" The problem with this is that Luke got it wrong. Lev 12:2–8 says it is *the woman* who has given birth who must offer sacrifice to be purified after childbirth, a lamb and a turtledove if she can afford it, or two turtledoves or pigeons if she cannot. Luke clearly is not going on firsthand information here but has adduced what he thinks must have been the sacrifice from his incorrect understanding of the Levitical law.

Had Luke a greater understanding of Palestinian Jewish life he would have realized that Joseph and his family were not poor. As Shimon Gibson points out:

> Joseph clearly possessed the financial means to cover the costs of traveling to Jerusalem to ensure that Jesus was presented in the Temple . . . and even to celebrating Passover there on an annual basis (Luke 2:41: "Now every year his parents went to Jerusalem for the festival of the Passover"). The cost of traveling in those days was exorbitant and could not have been undertaken by everyone. Not only was there a loss of earnings for the period the family was away from home, but food had to be bought along the way, and inns and road tolls had to be paid for. Jerusalem was an expensive city to stay in and accommodations were dear, especially at the time of festivities. Hence, the family of Jesus cannot have been poor.[69]

In Mark there is the account of Levi son of Alphaeus, a tax collector in Capernaum who left his toll booth and followed Jesus. Later Levi hosted a meal for Jesus shared by other tax collectors in which they all reclined to eat.[70] Although this type of tax collector was not at the top of the bureaucratic pyramid, Levi was wealthy enough to have a reasonably large house, one spacious enough for reclining benches and large enough to host a number of people for an elaborate meal. Clearly Levi (or Matthew, as the name is in the First Gospel) was a member of the retainer

---

69. Gibson, *Final Days of Jesus*, 4.

70. Mark 2:15. In the equivalent verses in Matt 9:10 and Luke 5:29, the Greek text says that Jesus and other others reclined at the meal, although some biblical translations incorrectly use the term "sit."

class. As a kinsman of Jesus (see above), it suggests that Joseph's family were members of the retainer class.

Another passage also hints at Jesus' higher economic status. In Mark 2:23–26 Jesus watches as his disciples pluck ears of grain from the fields on the Sabbath. Mosaic law permitted the poor to do this. Jesus' failure to join in this activity may indicate that he did not qualify as poor and thus was not allowed to pluck grain under the law.[71]

An even more direct reference to Jesus' economic status has been rejected by modern biblical scholars, despite the fact it comes from one of our earliest witnesses, the Apostle Paul. In 2 Cor 8:2–7 Paul praises the church in Macedonia for contributing, despite their poverty, to the collection of money for the relief of the Jerusalem church. Then, in verse 9, he writes: "For you know the generous act of our Lord Jesus Christ, that though he was rich, yet for your sakes he became poor, so that by his poverty you might become rich." Modern scholars opine that 2 Cor 8:9 is a theological metaphor and "rich" is a reference to Christ's pre-existence, citing Phil 2:6–8 on Jesus: "who, though he was in the form of God, . . . but emptied himself, taking the form of a slave, being born in human likeness. And being found in human form, he humbled himself and became obedient to the point of death, even death on a cross."[72]

However, George Wesley Buchanan pointed out that Phil 2:6–11 is thought to be a non-Pauline hymn and thus has no relationship whatsoever to the passage in 2 Cor 8:9. Looking solely at the *context* of the 2 Corinthians passage, particularly the direct comparison to the monetary contribution of the church in Macedonia, he concluded it meant just what it said: that Jesus had been rich and gave away his wealth, a practice known in Jesus' time, notably by the Essenes.[73] This is precisely what Jesus urges the rich young man in Mark 10:21 to do and what may be implied by Peter's statement that follows: "Look, we have left everything and followed you."

The term "rich" in 2 Cor 8:9 is an exaggeration. The truly rich were wealthy estate owners and aristocrats, the top 1 percent to 2 percent of the population. But if Jesus came from a family that was wealthier than

---

71. Casey, *Aramaic Sources*, 142.
72. Buchanan, "Jesus and the Upper Class," 196–97.
73. Ibid., 206–7.

over 90 percent of the population, as most of the retainer class were, the peasant and artisan classes might think of him as "rich."

An even more direct line of evidence gives a powerful indication that Jesus and his siblings lived above the peasant level of subsistence. In describing peasant health in first-century Palestine, biblical scholar Richard L. Rohrbaugh writes:

> Infant mortality rates have been estimated at 30 percent in many peasant societies, and that may well have been the case in first-century CE Palestine . . . Children were the first to suffer from disease, malnutrition, and poverty . . . About 60 percent of those who survived their first year of life were dead by age sixteen . . . For most lower-class people who did make it to adulthood, health would have been atrocious. By age thirty, the majority suffered from internal parasites, rotting teeth, and bad eyesight. Most had lived with the debilitating results of protein deficiency since childhood. Parasites were especially prevalent . . . If infant mortality rates, the age structure of the population, and pathological evidence from skeletal remains can be taken as indicators, malnutrition was a constant threat as well.[74]

As Rohrbaugh also points out, "Obviously disease and high death rates were not evenly spread across all elements of the population *but rather fell disproportionately upon the lower classes* [my italics] of both city and village."[75]

Using the numbers quoted by Rohrbaugh, a woman who gave birth to eight children (a typical number of live births for village women in India in pre-modern times) could expect to see six of them die before they became adults. But amidst this dismal picture of infant and childhood disease, malnutrition, and death, Joseph's family produced five sons and at least two daughters, *seven children at least, who survived to maturity*. The survival of so many children in Joseph's family is powerful and direct evidence that its members did not suffer from the privation that characterized the lives of first-century Palestinian peasants.

The nutritional problems of Palestinian peasants would also have effected their intelligence and certain motor abilities, as a number of studies have shown, particularly when there was malnutrition or undernutrition

---

74. Rohrbaugh, "Social Location of the Markan Audience," 154.
75. Ibid.

in the first two and a half years of life.[76] The apathetic, unintelligent victim of chronic malnutrition bears little resemblance either to Jesus or to his brother James. James led the Jerusalem Christian community, a community that included scribes and priests, for over thirty years and, according to the Jewish historian Josephus, was so important that he was executed by the high priest and the Sanhedrin.[77] Nor does such a picture make sense for Jesus' disciple kinsmen, or his other brothers who conducted their ministry throughout the Mediterranean world.

One must conclude from this evidence that Joseph and his brothers were prosperous enough to produce numbers of healthy and intelligent sons and daughters, in marked contrast to peasant families in first-century Palestine. Their membership in the retainer class would fit in this context. Joseph, as the oldest son in Jacob's family and thus entitled to a double portion of his father's inheritance, and claiming a lineage of great ascribed honor in its descent from King David, would have been a very prestigious and desirable candidate for marriage.

---

76. See, for example, Stoch and Smythe, "Undernutrition during Infancy," 278–89; Grantham-McGregor and Ani, "Undernutrition and Mental Development," 1–18. Most of the studies mentioned in this second article use an I.Q. of 80 as "normal."

77. Josephus, *Ant.* 20:197–203.

2

The Genealogies of Jesus and the Family of Mary

THE MOST RECENT LINEAGE SEGMENT IN THE GOSPEL OF MATTHEW

IN THE PREVIOUS CHAPTER we looked at how two of the four independent genealogical sources were incorrectly combined and how the post-David genealogy in the Gospel of Luke could be untangled to discover the real ancestry of Jesus' ostensible father Joseph. Let's now look at another of these genealogical sources, the list of eight names just before Joseph's father in Matthew's genealogy (Matt 1:13–16): Abiud, Eliakim, Azor, Zadok, Achim, Eliud, Eleazar, Matthan. These eight names are said to represent the generations between Zerubbabel and Joseph's father Jacob. But since Zerubbabel lived over 500 years before Jesus, there are clearly not enough names here. Also, Abiud, supposedly the son of Zerubbabel in Matthew's genealogy, is not listed as a son of Zerubbabel in 1 Chr 3:19–20.

So where did this list come from? I think these eight names were on a written list, on which the name Matthan was followed by the name Joseph and that the list was carried to Antioch by Christians fleeing the Romans in 66–70 CE. Antioch is where the Gospel of Matthew is thought to have been written.[1] The writer of Matthew (who wished to associate his Gospel with the disciple Matthew but was not himself Matthew),[2] getting this written list without any detailed information about it, also knew of another tradition likewise brought to Antioch by Jerusalem Christians. This other tradition was that Joseph's father had been named Jacob or that James the Lord's brother had been named after his grandfather Jacob (see chapter 1). The writer of Matthew trusted this oral tradition as much

---

1. Meier, "Antioch," 15, 22–27.
2. Bauckham, *Eyewitnesses*, 112.

as he trusted the written list. He probably assumed that the written list contained a copying error and that the name Jacob had been inadvertently left out. Crediting both of his separate sources, oral and written, the Gospel writer inserted "begat (or the father of) Jacob" after Matthan and before "begat Joseph."

As we saw in the previous chapter, however, the names on this written list were not the ancestors of Joseph, Mary's husband. Who are they, then? For a start, the name Abiud is a form of Abihu, who was a son of the first high priest Aaron. In later Jewish tradition Abihu and his brother were designated as captains of the temple or *seganim*.[3] Rather than being a royal name of the line of David, Abiud is a priestly name. Other names on this list are also priestly names. Abiud's son is Eliakim. A priest named Eliakim is mentioned in Neh 12:41 in the fifth century BCE, too early to be the Eliakim on Matthew's list. Eliakim is a variant of the name Yaqim, and in Matthew's list Achim (that is, Yaqim) is also the son of Zadok. Zadok was the high priest under David's son, Solomon, and all individuals named Zadok in the Hebrew Bible were priests.[4] Achim was evidently named for his great-grandfather Eliakim.

The name of Eleazar, Achim's grandson, is usually, but not exclusively, a priestly name and was popular among Egyptian Jews during the Ptolemaic and early Roman periods.[5] Finally on Matthew's list, Matthan is a form of Mattathias or Matthias. It is the name of the priest who fathered the Hasmoneans, the name of several priestly ancestors and relatives of the priestly historian Josephus, the name of a high priest in the last year of King Herod's life, and the name of several high priests of the house of Ananus.[6]

If the writer of Matthew had merely made this list up, surely he would not have used such priestly, rather than Davidic, names. So where did this list come from?

Records of the genealogies of priests were kept in the temple in Jerusalem, and so were the genealogical records of women in priestly families. If these records were destroyed, as some may have been in the

---

3. Jeremias, *Jerusalem*, 162.

4. Sanders, *Judaism*, 171. For Zadok as Solomon's high priest see 1 Kgs 1:38, 39; 2:35.

5. Stern, "Relations between Judea and Rome," 21, n. 119 (in Hebrew); but see Ilan, *Lexicon*, 70, n. 3. For its popularity in Egypt see Johnson, *Genealogies*, 180.

6. For the Hasmoneans, see chapter 1. For Josephus's genealogy see Josephus, *Life* 1:4–5, 8. For the high priest Matthias son of Theophilus see Josephus *Ant.* 17:78, 165–67. For the high priests of the house of Ananus see Smallwood, "High Priests and Politics," 32.

Macabbean wars of the second century BCE, efforts were made to reconstruct them from the surviving records.[7] The names from Abiud to Matthan in Matthew appear to be one of these lists, a priestly genealogy, or the genealogy of a woman in a priestly family. As such it would have been a matter of public record and could have been copied by a member of the early Christian community in Jerusalem, a community that included both scribes and priests, and then later carried to Antioch.

In the early centuries of Christianity there were a number of claims by church fathers that Mary the mother of Jesus was of Davidic descent, for the obvious reason that if Jesus was not the son of Joseph, then he could not be the Davidic messiah unless he had received a Davidic bloodline through his mother. But there was another persistent ancient tradition, one roundly condemned by early church fathers who wanted to emphasize Jesus' Davidic descent. This alternate tradition was that Mary was of priestly or Levitical descent. Hyppolytus (fourth century CE), Origin (born about 185 CE), Ephraem the Syrian (died 375 CE), and Augustine knew of this tradition, although the last three denied it.[8] Modern scholars have opined that this tradition of priestly descent had its roots in the first chapter of the Gospel of Luke, which features Mary's kinswoman Elizabeth who was a member of a priestly family and was married to a priest.[9] But, given the high degree of intermarriage in priestly families, it is indeed likely that if Mary's relatives were members of priestly families, she would be as well.

One asks therefore, if Mary were from a priestly family and this list of eight names in the Gospel of Matthew were a list of her ancestors, why does it have Joseph, the husband of Mary on the list? In Matthew's genealogy all the names are in the formal style of the Hebrew Bible: A begat B begat C and so forth. The genealogy ends with "Matthan begat Jacob, and Jacob begat Joseph, the husband of Mary; of whom was born Jesus, who was called Christ."[10] I believe the written list originally went: Matthan begat Joseph and Joseph begat Mary of her was begotten Jesus. The writer of Matthew, thinking that he had a list of the ancestors of Joseph Mary's husband, believed the phrase "Joseph begat Mary" was an error and replaced

---

7. Josephus, *Ag. Ap.* 1:30–36; Jeremias, *Jerusalem*, 214–15, 216, 283; Johnson, *Genealogies*, 99–101.

8. Brown et al., *Mary*, 154 n. 345, 261.

9. Brown et al., *Mary*, 153–54.

10. Matt 1:15–16 KJV.

it with "Joseph the husband of Mary" at the same time he added "Jacob" for Joseph's father between "Matthan" and "Joseph." Then, satisfied that he had corrected the copying errors he believed were on this list, he added it to his larger genealogy.

THE NAMES OF MARY'S FATHER, GRANDPARENTS, AND SISTER

This means that the Joseph on Matthew's original uncorrected list was not the husband of Mary, but her father. Joseph was the secondmost common name among male Jews in Palestine during this time period, and so it is not extraordinary that these two men should have the same name.[11] An earlier scholar, H. A. Blair, noted that the purported name of Mary's father in the mid-second-century *Protevangelium of James* was Joachim, which means "may God set up," and that Joseph means "may God add," two quite similar meanings that might have led to confusion as the name was passed down in early Christian tradition.[12] We will get back to these names later in the chapter.

If the recent genealogy in the Gospel of Matthew is actually the ancestry of Mary's father Joseph, then this Joseph's father (that is, Mary's grandfather) was named Matthan. In the third century the Christian writer Julius Africanus, in an attempt to reconcile the genealogies of Matthew and Luke, wrote that Jacob the son of Matthan (from Matthew's genealogy) and Eli the son of Matthat (from Luke's genealogy), were brothers on the mother's side, and that the name of the mother was Estha or Esther.[13] Both Matthan and Matthat are forms of the name Matthew, and I think Africanus, who had some Palestinian background,[14] used an early Christian tradition from Palestine that the wife of Matthan was named Esther. Another ancient source, a text fragment known as the Madrid Codex 82, has the early Christian writer Hyppolytus quoting Epiphanius as saying Joseph's daughters were Esther and Maria.[15] I think in this case

---

11. Ilan, *Lexicon*, 56, table 7.

12. Blair, "Matthew 1,16," 153 n.

13. Wallraff, *Julius Africanus Chronographiae*, 273. Julius Africanus then goes on to say that after Eli died his brother Jacob took her (his own mother?—there is no other woman named) to wife and had a son Joseph who, according to the law of levirate marriage, was the actual son of Jacob and legal son of Eli.

14. Ibid., xv.

15. Blinzler, *Brüder und Schwestern Jesu*, 37.

the Joseph in question is not the husband of Mary but her father and that Joseph the son of Matthan had another daughter, Esther, named for her paternal grandmother. This would be in line with the practice, mentioned in the previous chapter, of naming a daughter for her grandmother. Since Esther is named first in the ancient Christian fragment she is likely to have been the older of the two sisters. She is probably the sister who stood, along with Mary of Clopas and Mary Magdalene, with Mary the mother of Jesus at the cross (see John 19:25).

THE NAME OF JOSEPH'S FATHER IN THE GOSPEL OF LUKE

Identifying Joseph, Mary's father, as the son of Matthan or Matthew brings up another question: Who is the Heli (or Eli) named as Joseph's father in the Gospel of Luke? It is known that Luke used a number of sources in composing his Gospel, some of them orally transmitted. Cognitive and social psychologists studying the transmission of oral information have found that names fare poorly in this process, and often less familiar names are changed to more familiar ones.[16] Because of this characteristic feature of oral transmission, Heli or Eli may be a more familiar version of a less familiar original name or nickname. When Luke encountered the name Joseph ben Heli or Eli, he would have assumed that this Joseph was Mary's husband and that the father of Mary's husband was named Heli or Eli. Not unlike the writer of Matthew, Luke must have felt this name was from a reliable source, and so he added it to the written list he had acquired (see chapter 1), a list that probably originally ended with Matthat (see table 3).

Ancient Christian tradition associates Mary's birth and childhood with the town of Sepphoris in Galilee.[17] Both the first-century Jewish historian Josephus and rabbinic sources mention a priest from Sepphoris late in the reign of King Herod named Joseph ben Elim or Elem or Ellem (Joseph son of the mute) who substituted for his relative, Matthias ben Theophilus, as high priest on Yom Kippur.[18]

---

16. Bartlett, *Remembering*, 175; Allport and Postman, *Psychology of Rumor*, 84, 124–25; Campbell, "Systematic Error," 347–52; Higham, "Experimental Study," 51.

17. Ward, "Sepphoris in Sacred Geography," 396–97.

18. Josephus, *Ant.* 17:165–66; Miller, *Sepphoris*, 63–74; Schürer, *History of the Jewish People*, 229 n. 7.

26 THE THREE PILLARS

The story of Joseph ben Elim is found in the rabbinic literature and in the account of the Jewish historian Josephus.[19] The night before Yom Kippur, or Day of Atonement, the holiest day of the Jewish year, the high priest, Matthias ben Theophilus, had a dream that made him ritually unclean. Because of this his relative, Joseph ben Elim, substituted for Matthias in the temple sacrifices the next day.

Beyond the regular daily sacrifices, on the Day of Atonement the high priest was presented with two goats.[20] One of the goats was chosen to be sacrificed to God while the other became the scapegoat. During the course of the temple services on Yom Kippur the high priest entered the holy of holies. The holy of holies was forbidden to all but the high priest, and even he was allowed to enter it only on the Day of Atonement. The high priest also killed a bull and the goat chosen for God and brought their blood into the holy of holies.

According to rabbinic traditions, Joseph ben Elim wished to retain his place as high priest after Yom Kippur by paying for the animals sacrificed that day, but King Herod refused this request and instead reinstated Matthias ben Theophilus.[21] Matthias did not remain as high priest for long, however, because King Herod held Matthias partly responsible for the destruction of a golden eagle that the king had erected over the temple gate.[22]

There is a connection in the rabbinic literature between the designated substitute for the high priest and the office of *segan* (plural *seganim*), probably because in the last decades of the temple's existence one of the duties of the *segan* was to substitute for the high priest. But in Joseph ben Elim's time the duties of the *segan* did not include substitution.[23] Joseph ben Elim happened to be the closest relative of Matthias ben Theophilus participating in the temple service during the week before Yom Kippur and was consequently designated as Matthias's substitute should the need arise.[24]

Given the genealogical likelihood that Mary was from a priestly family, that her father was named Joseph, in Lukan oral tradition the son of someone named Heli or Eli or something that sounded like it (such as

19. *t. Yoma* 1:14; *y. Yoma* 1, 38c–d; *b. Yoma* 12b–13a; Josephus, *Ant.* 17:165–66.
20. See Schauss, *Jewish Festivals*, 125–40.
21. Miller, *Sepphoris*, 64–65.
22. Josephus, *Ant.*17:155–57, 164, 167.
23. Miller, *Sepphoris*, 80–88.
24. Ibid., 87.

Elim), and the ancient tradition of Sepphoris as Mary's place of origin, this Joseph is very likely Mary's father. The formal name of Mary's grandfather, Matthan (Matthew or Matthias), was also the name of Joseph ben Elim's close relative, Matthias ben Theophilus. In prominent Jewish families during this period, it was increasingly common for a personal name to appear multiple times in the same family through several generations.[25]

Other fragments of early Christian traditions may also hearken back to the connection between Joseph ben Elim and Mary. The *Protevangelium of James* contains the story that Mary was raised in the temple's holy of holies overseen by the high priest.[26] Another tradition in Eusebius, quoting the second-century Christian Jewish writer Hegesippus, says that James the Lord's brother was allowed into the sacred precinct of the temple.[27] Epiphanius says that James entered the holy of holies once a year like the high priest.[28] The traditions that connect Mary and her son James to the temple's holy of holies are impossible in terms of Jewish law, but they may have developed from a vestigial memory of Mary's high-priestly connection, a connection associated with the one time each year the high priest was allowed to enter the holy of holies—Yom Kippur. It should be noted that even people who merely came from a high-priestly family are termed "high priest" in Josephus and in Acts, and that former high priests retained the use of that title.[29]

JOSEPH BEN ELIM'S ANCESTORS

Tal Ilan, in her exhaustive compendium of Jewish names in late antiquity, has suggested that Elem (Elim) was a nickname rather than a formal name.[30] As she points out, nicknames often masqueraded as a father's name. They were common in Second Temple times and used extensively because there were so few formal names as a result of the prevalent patronymic naming pattern.[31] Rachel Hachlili notes that for a priest, nick-

25. Hachlili, "Goliath Family," 53; idem, "Names and Nicknames," 192–94; idem, "Hebrew Names," 88.
26. *Prot. Jas.* 8–16; see Cullmann and Higgins, "Protevangelium," 378–83.
27. Eusebius, *Eccl. Hist.* 2:23.
28. Epiphanius, *Pan.* 78:7.
29. Levine, *Jerusalem*, 354–55.
30. Ilan, *Lexicon*, 361 n. 3 under Elem.
31. Naveh, "Nameless People," 113; Hachlili, "Hebrew Names," 86, 88, 94–96; Ilan, *Lexicon*, 46.

names derived from a disability indicated that a person could not serve in the temple.[32] Since Joseph ben Elim did serve in the temple, he was not the source of this nickname.

However, ben Elim or Elem could have started as an ancestral nickname that became a family name. Hachlili points out that "a surname could be a nickname given to one (or more) of the ancestors by virtue of ... physical characteristic and defects... Many families are known whose nickname evolved into a family name."[33] This was the case for the Goliath family of Jericho, known for their unusual height.[34] Also, Josephus at times refers to various descendants of the high-priestly house of Boethus as "son of Boethus," although some were simply male descendants of Boethus, not his sons. If ben Elim or Elem is a descriptive nickname that became a family name, its use implies a notable mute in the family's ancestry.

There was such a notable mute, the Jewish high priest Alcimus (his Greek name, which means valiant), who was appointed by the Seleucid rulers of Palestine and served in Jerusalem between 163 or 162 and 159 BCE.[35] According to 1 Maccabees, Alcimus died while tearing down part of the wall of the temple that separated the Jews from the Gentiles: "at that time Alcimus was stricken and his work was hindered; his mouth was stopped and he was paralyzed, so that he could no longer say a word or give commands concerning his house. And Alcimus died at that time in great agony."[36] Josephus reports that after his stroke Alcimus underwent torments for many days.[37] Thus before he died Alcimus was indeed mute, and the fact that he had a stroke implies that he was of advanced years, probably in his fifties or sixties, when he died.

Alcimus's Hebrew name was Yaqim or Jakim. The name Yaqim (in the form of Eliakim) also appears on Matthew's list as an ancestor of Joseph (both "El" and "Jo" are prefixes that refer to God). The Eliakim on Matthew's list, grandfather of Zadok and great-grandfather of his namesake Achim, was probably born about 215 BCE, using twenty-four years per generation (as in the previous chapter) and an estimated birth of Joseph at 46 or 47 BCE. This fits very well with the estimated age of the

---

32. Hachlili, "Hebrew Names," 105, 109, 111.
33. Ibid., 93.
34. Hachlili, "Goliath Family," 31–65.
35. VanderKam, *Joshua*, 226–45.
36. 1 Macc 9:55–56.
37. Josephus, *Ant.* 12:413.

high priest Yaqim/Alcimus at his death. By this estimate, Zadok would have been born about 160 BCE, during his grandfather's high priesthood. It is easy to see why the grandson of the high priest would have been given this quintessential high-priestly name, and why he in turn named his own son after his high-priestly grandfather.

Jakim or Alcimus is thought to be the high priest Joakim or Jehoiakim son of Hilkiah son of Shallum mentioned in the Jewish apocryphal work of that time period, Baruch.[38] It is likely that at least part of the surviving temple records of this family did indeed get destroyed (probably by the Hasmoneans—see below) as happened during this period and mentioned earlier in this chapter, and the early names Hilkiah and Shallum were left off the reconstructed list (see figure 2).

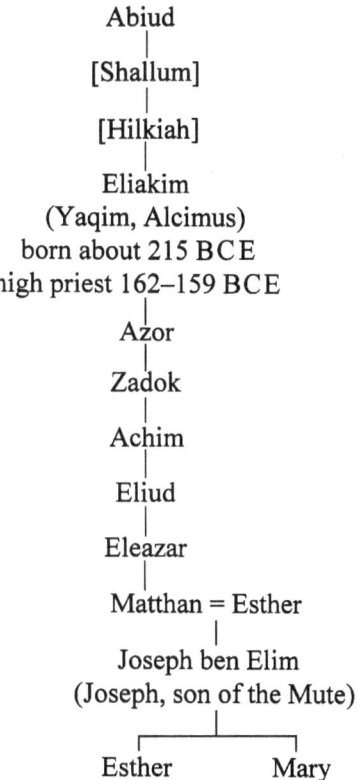

FIGURE 2. Ancestors and family of Mary. Names in brackets are from Bar 1:7.

---

38. Bar 1:7; see VanderKam Joshua, 48 n. 10, 239 n. 345.

There is an even more direct thread linking the name Yaqim to Mary. The name of Mary's father in the *Protevangelium of James* is Joachim,[39] a variant of this name, the one used in Bar 1:7. As mentioned earlier, the names Joachim and Joseph have similar meanings, and it is likely that these two high priests in Mary's ancestry became confused in the Aramaic oral tradition about her, part of which eventually found its way into the *Protevangelium of James*.

Josephus says that Alcimus was a descendent of Aaron, but not from the high-priestly family itself, and puts the appointment of Alcimus as high priest at the time the ostensible high priest Onas IV fled to Egypt.[40] Given the similarity of the names, the fact that he was appointed high priest in the first place, and that he had a following among at least some of the Jews, I think it is possible that Yaqim/Alcimus claimed descent from a namesake, Joiakim, the son of the first high priest after the exile, Jeshua.[41]

YAKIM/ALCIMUS AND THE HASMONEANS

Alcimus is vilified in all the historical sources available to us—1 Maccabees, 2 Maccabees, and Josephus's *Antiquities of the Jews*—because he was the bitter enemy of Judah the Maccabee (Josephus was a descendent of the Hasmoneans through a maternal line[42]). Although Alcimus is regarded by most historians as a Hellenizer,[43] he may only have been so in a political, not a religious sense, for as Jonathan A. Goldstein points out, the Seleucids, "eager for peace in Judaea, could have appointed only a pious Jew to the high priesthood."[44] Many pious Jews, undoubtedly including Alcimus, regarded the Seleucids as lawful rulers; thus it was a grave sin to rebel against them.[45] This attitude made him and his followers, who probably included the majority of the people,[46] opponents of Judah the Maccabee and the rest of the Hasmoneans, who rejected the claims of the

---

39. *Prot. Jas.* 1–6; see Cullmann and Higgins, "Protevangelium," 374–77.
40. Josephus, *Ant.* 12:387; 20:235; VanderKam, *Joshua*, 227–28.
41. Neh 12:10, 26.
42. Josephus, *Life* 1, 4.
43. VanderKam, *Joshua*, 227–29; Eshel, *Dead Sea Scrolls*, 54.
44. Goldstein, *II Maccabees*, 481.
45. Goldstein, *I Maccabees*, 64–65.
46. Eshel, *Dead Sea Scrolls*, 76.

Seleucids to be lawful rulers of the Jews. Josephus concedes that Alcimus had "a great body of men and an army about him" and that forces loyal to Alcimus battled those loyal to Judah the Maccabee.[47] In short, it was a bitter civil war, with both sides vying for approval and support from the Seleucid overlord.

After the takeover of Jerusalem by the Hasmoneans in the person of Judah's brother Jonathan, in 152 BCE,[48] the descendants and family of Alcimus would likely have fled the city into Seleucid-dominated territory outside of Hasmonean control. Archaeological excavations have revealed the existence of a Seleucid fort at Sepphoris in Galilee, built by Antiochus III or Antiochus IV. These excavations have also revealed late second-century Jewish ritual baths and a Hebrew inscription on pottery dating to the late second century BCE, even before the city's takeover by the Hasmoneans.[49] Sepphoris, then, Seleucid-dominated but with a Jewish population, would have been a good refuge for the family and descendants of Yaqim/Alcimus in the mid-second century BCE. By the time the Hasmoneans took control of Sepphoris in about 100 BCE, the family probably felt enough time had passed that it was safe to remain there.

JOSEPH BEN ELIM AND THE HOUSE OF BOETHUS

Although Joseph ben Elim came from Sepphoris, Josephus says his relative Matthias ben Theophilus was a Jerusalemite, although we don't know how long he or his family had been residents of Jerusalem.[50] Matthias succeeded Simon the son of Boethus as high priest. Simon, or more likely his father Boethus, came from Alexandria in Egypt and may have been a descendent of the Zadokite priest Onias IV who was driven out of Jerusalem and fled to Egypt in 164 or 162 BCE, an event quite possibly related to the appointment of Alcimus to the high priesthood.[51] Some scholars have thought that Matthias ben Theophilus was Simon's son-in-law, but others,

---

47. Josephus, *Ant.* 12:398–99.
48. VanderKam, *Joshua*, 242–45; Horsley, *Galilee: History, Politics, People*, 36.
49. Chancey and Meyers, "How Jewish Was Sepphoris?," 18–33, 61.
50. Josephus, *Ant.* 17:78.
51. Hengel, *"Hellenization" of Judaea*, 14; Josephus, *Ant.* 12:387–88, 20:235–36. For an interpretation of these passages in Josephus compared to the version in 2 Macc. see VanderKam, *Joshua*, 214–21.

more persuasively I think, have rejected this idea.[52] If, like his relative Joseph ben Elim, Matthias was a descendant of Alcimus, his appointment by Herod would have been seen as an anti-Hasmonean gesture, one of many Herod made in his reign, particularly after Herod executed his two half-Hasmonean sons in about 8 BCE (see below). Rather than being related to the house of Boethus, I think Matthias and Joseph ben Elim may have been seen as rivals to that family, particularly if their ancestor Alcimus had supplanted Simon's ancestor Onias IV.

The house of Boethus was one of the four great high-priestly houses mentioned in the Talmud and in Josephus, the others being Hanan (Annas or Ananus), Kathros, and Ishmael ben Phiabi.[53] According to Josephus, the high priest Simon surnamed Kathros was in fact a member of the house of Boethus.[54] The name Kathros may even be a variant of Caiaphas,[55] the surname of the high priest who, with his father-in-law Annas or Ananus, arrested Jesus and sent him to the Roman prefect Pontius Pilate, who in turn executed him.

THE WEDDING AT CANA AND THE FAMILY OF MARY'S SISTER ESTHER

Cana, site of Jesus' first miracle in the Gospel of John,[56] has now been securely identified as Khirbit Qana, about nine miles north of Nazareth and about four or five miles north of Sepphoris. Archaeological investigations at Khirbit Qana have discovered several reasonably large early Roman-era houses with plastered walls and courtyards, a sherd with writing on it, the remnants of stone vessels (used for ritual bathing), and in the lower part of the town caves containing a Christian shrine of Byzantine age with gold on marble.[57]

---

52. For various interpretations of the family of Boethus see: Stern, "Jewish Society," 604–08; Smallwood, "High Priests and Politics," 33–34; Schwartz, *Agrippa I*, 185–89; Schwartz, *Judaean Politics*, 59–60; Kokkinos, *Dynasty*, 218–22; VanderKam, *Joshua*, 407, 412–16.

53. Jeremias, *Jerusalem*, 194–95.

54. Josephus, *Ant.* 19:297.

55. Brody, "Caiaphas and Cantheras," 190–95; see also VanderKam, *Joshua*, 444–47, 449–51.

56. John 2:1–12.

57. Edwards, "Khirbet Qana," 101–32; Richardson, *Building Jewish*, 55–71.

Several of the earliest surviving texts of the wedding of Cana, such as the Codex Sinaiticus, do not mention Jesus' disciples in John 2:12, while the early Christian writers Chrysostom and Epiphanius do mention his mother and brothers in relation to this story.[58] Most likely the wedding occurred before Jesus' ministry for in verse 4 Jesus says, "My hour has not yet come," and his disciples were a later addition to the list of Jesus, his mother, and his brothers.

This story has some peculiar features in it. Had the story simply been constructed to illustrate Jesus' first miracle, one would expect a man or men to be the primary actors, for example, the groom or his father asking Jesus to help them. Instead, it is Jesus' mother who takes the initiative when the wine runs out, and even orders the servants in the house around, and they obey her! Imagine a random female guest attending a wedding reception in someone's house and taking responsibility for the lack of beverages, as well as ordering the catering staff to do whatever her son told them to do. The staff, if they knew what was good for them, would ignore her. Now imagine that, instead of a random guest, we have the groom's aunt, who is also the sister of the mistress of the house, doing the same thing. The servants of the house, if they knew what was good for them, would do what she and her son (the groom's cousin) told them to do.

This suggested familial relationship, that Mary's sister Esther was the mother of the groom, would explain why Mary and her family, namely Jesus and his brothers, were invited to the wedding at all, nine miles away from Nazareth and past Sepphoris to the north, and also why Mary was so concerned about the success of the wedding feast and with it the honor of her sister's family, why Mary could order the servants of the house about with impunity, why they obeyed her without question, and why Jesus, on being told by Mary that "They have no wine," replies to her: "What has this concern *of yours* [my italics] to do with me?" He is actually saying: "These are your relatives. The honor of my family, that is, the family of Joseph the *tektōn*, is not involved here." But Jesus, responding to his kinship obligations, saw to the wine anyway. The fact that Jesus and his family are relatives of the groom is not mentioned because the Gospel story is about Jesus working his first miracle, not about his family relationships. If Jesus had been seen as simply doing something for his

---

58. Bernheim, *James*, 83.

family, the impact of this miracle would have been greatly lessened in the minds of the first- and second-century audiences who heard the story.

Putting this story into a kinship context also gives us some information about Mary's family, or at least the family into which her sister married. The presence of the stone jars for ritual cleansing indicates a devout, possibly a priestly family, likely since Mary and Esther were priest's daughters. The family was wealthy enough to have servants and a wedding feast that lasted at least three days (John 2:1) but not so wealthy that they could provide enough wine. Not poor priests, but not rich ones either, this family could have occupied one of the courtyard houses excavated at Khirbit Qana. Broadly speaking, they would fit into the retainer class suggested in the previous chapter for Joseph's family.

THE BETROTHAL OF MARY TO JOSEPH

It is not hard to imagine that Joseph ben Elim could have become acquainted with the family of Jacob while Jacob and his sons were working on building projects in Sepphoris in the last two decades of the first century BCE, late in King Herod's lifetime. Their Davidic descent would have given Jacob's family great ascribed honor, and daughters of priests did at times marry into non-priestly families. However, one wonders why Joseph ben Elim, whose ancestors had been such bitter enemies of the Hasmoneans, betrothed his younger daughter into a family who had been supporters of the Hasmonean monarchy or why Jacob, with his pro-Hasmonean ancestors, would have betrothed his oldest son to a girl descended from the bitterly anti-Hasmonean high priest Alcimus. The historical context may shed some light on this problem.

Both the Gospels of Matthew and Luke put Jesus' birth in the lifetime of King Herod, who died not long before Passover in 4 BCE.[59] Daniel R. Schwartz convincingly puts the fateful dream of Matthias ben Theopolis a few days before a full lunar eclipse on the night of 15/16 September 5 BCE and thus the Yom Kippur in which Joseph ben Elim served as high priest on 12/13 September of that year.[60] This means that Joseph and Mary would have been betrothed before Joseph ben Elim served as high

---

59. Hoehner, "Date of the Death of Herod," 101–11.

60. Schwartz, "Joseph ben Illem," 157–66. This September lunar eclipse was a full eclipse and visible for 220 minutes starting at 8:50 P.M., while the other eclipse often mentioned, in the following March, was a small partial eclipse visible in Jerusalem only between 1:45 and 4:00 in the morning when everyone was asleep!

priest. The census, which marks Jesus' birth in the Gospel of Luke, in fact occurred in 6/7 CE.[61] The census is a landmark event, and such events often get shifted in oral tradition to more appropriate settings.[62] I think that the census originally was part of the story of Jesus in the temple at aged twelve, but that it was moved to the more notable event, his birth, much as the story of the star and the magi, originally set up to two years after the birth (see Matt 2:16), now graces Christmas pageants around the world. If the story of Jesus in the temple coincided with the Passover at the time of the census in 7 CE, his birth would have been in the last two-thirds of 7 BCE or the first third of 6 BCE (there is no year zero). Joseph and Mary would thus have been betrothed in the latter part of 8 or the earlier part of 7 BCE.

In about 8 BCE King Herod executed his two sons who were descended from the Hasmonean royal dynasty on their mother's side.[63] These executions would have dashed any popular hopes for a resurrection of the Hasmonean dynasty through the maternal line, and at the same time raised expectations for the appearance of a Davidic ruler in the minds of those who had always regarded the Hasmoneans as illegitimate pretenders. A year or two after these executions, a conspiracy against Herod was uncovered, one that included another of Herod's sons, Antipater II, and the wife of Herod's brother Pheroras.[64] Connected to this conspiracy was a prophecy, made apparently by the Pharisees, that involved an expected messiah.[65]

Expectations of a king from the line of David, a messiah or "anointed one," had started with Zerubbabel in the sixth century BCE (see Zech 4:13, which refers to two anointed ones, Zerubbabel and his contemporary, the high priest Jeshua). However, these lay dormant for centuries, only to resurface as a form of opposition to the Hasmonean kings who were regarded by some Jews as illegitimate pretenders.[66] Such expectations grew as time went on, and by the final years of Herod's reign when the king's health was deteriorating, they were common in Palestinian Judaism, as

61. Schürer, *History of the Jewish People*, 399-427.
62. Henige, *Oral Historiography*, 103.
63. Josephus, *War* 1:538-51; *Ant.* 16:356-94; dates from Kokkinos, *Dynasty*, 215.
64. Josephus, *Ant.* 17:32-45.
65. Flusser, "'The House of David' on an Ossuary," 37-40; Kokkinos, *Dynasty*, 170-71, 173-74.
66. Collins, *Scepter*, 29-31, 49; see also Johnson, *Genealogies*, 115-38.

evidenced by material in the Dead Sea Scrolls and the messianic prophecy in the conspiracy against Herod in 7/6 BCE. The Davidic messiah is often referred to as a branch or shoot from the stump of Jessie in the ancient literature, including the Dead Sea Scrolls.[67] Another widely cited passage, Num 24:17: "a star shall come out of Jacob, and a scepter shall rise out of Israel" was also widely regarded as referring to this messiah.[68]

Although the most common expectation was for a military king of David's lineage as messiah, there were other messianic ideas, particularly that of a priestly "messiah of Aaron" who was featured so prominently in the Dead Sea Scrolls.[69] There is also evidence from documents found among the Dead Sea Scrolls and elsewhere that at least some first-century BCE Jews expected only one messiah who represented both the priestly and lay elements of Israel: "the root he [God] had planted to sprout from Israel and Aaron."[70]

Genealogically, a "messiah of Israel and Aaron" would descend from a Davidic line on the father's side and from a priestly line on the mother's, following the idea expressed as early as the early second century BCE by the Jewish sage ben Sirach that the covenant of David was from son to son only (Sir 45:25), "while the inheritance of Aaron belongs to his whole seed."[71]

Given the political unrest and the rising messianic expectations current about the time that Mary was betrothed to Joseph, the descent of Joseph from Zerubbabel and the Levitical descent of Mary, even the possibility that Mary and her father Joseph ben Elim were descended from the first post-exilic high priest Jeshua (see above)—the two anointed ones specifically referred to in the messianic prophecy in Zechariah—coupled with the interesting coincidence that the well-known prophetic passage in Num 24:17 mentions *Jacob*, also the name of Joseph's father, I can't help but wonder if Mary's priestly father betrothed her to Joseph, despite the ancestral political differences between the two families, because such

---

67. Collins, *Scepter*, 49–73.
68. Collins, *Scepter*, 61, 63–65, 67, 74, 78, 80, 105, 202–3; Johnson, *Genealogies*, 121.
69. Collins, *Scepter*, 74–101.
70. Wise and Tabor, "Messiah at Qumran," 60–65. The quote is from the Damascus Rule (CD 1:5–7).
71. Flusser, "Judaism and the Origins of Christianity," 257; see also Charles, "Fragments," 795.

a match would fulfill the genealogical requirements for and thus have the possibility of producing, a "messiah of Israel and Aaron."

If this seems an unlikely proposal, I will note that at the end of the twentieth century eight sets of Jewish parents in Israel agreed to turn over their prospective sons to be raised in isolation and ritual purity in order that they would qualify to sacrifice a red heifer and thus obtain its ashes to facilitate the re-establishment of the Jewish temple.[72] Such a re-establishment, many Jewish and Christian believers hold, would set the stage for the appearance, or reappearance, of the Messiah.

---

72. Gorenberg, *End of Days*, 145–46.

3

The Brothers and Sisters of Jesus and Their Role in the Early Church

Both the Gospels of Mark and John make it clear that the brothers of Jesus were not his followers in his lifetime. In John, Jesus' brothers urge him to go to Jerusalem for the Feast of Tabernacles (or Booths, held in the autumn) but he refuses to go with them. As John reports "for not even his brothers believed in him."[1] In Mark the division between Jesus and his family is far more visceral. Jesus' mother and brothers come to where he is healing in Capernaum and try to take him home because they think he is out of his mind. Jesus rejects them saying that those who do the will of God are his brother, sister, and mother.[2] Later in Mark, Jesus says that prophets are not without honor except among their own kin and in their own house.[3]

Nonetheless, the brothers and mother of Jesus are present in the upper room with the disciples and other followers of Jesus on the day of Pentecost fifty days after the first Easter.[4] The only clue we have for this change in attitude is from Paul's first letter to the Corinthians in which he lists those who had seen the risen Christ: first Cephas (Peter), then the twelve disciples, then 500 brethren at one time, then James, then all the apostles.[5] This list does not agree with the stories of the sightings of the risen Jesus in the Gospels, which commence with an initial appearance to Mary Magdalene and Jesus' sisters, then an appearance to Peter, and then appearances first to ten and later to eleven disciples in the upper room in Jerusalem and to seven disciples in Galilee.[6]

---

1. John 7:2–10 (quote in verse 5).
2. Mark 3:21, 31–35.
3. Mark 6:4.
4. Acts 1:14.
5. 1 Cor 15:5–7.
6. Matt 28:9–10; Luke 24:34; John 20:19–29; 21:1–23.

The Gospel of Mark does report that the sisters of Jesus were his followers during his lifetime, however. In Mark 15:40 both Salome and Mary the mother of James the lesser and Joses are said to have followed Jesus in Galilee and ministered to him. Also in Mark, Salome and her sister Mary stand in view of the cross and are present at the tomb, although in that Gospel the women see only a young man dressed in white, presumably an angel, but do not see the risen Jesus.[7] In Luke Jesus' sister Mary and other women see two men (again, presumably angels). His sister Mary is an actual witness to the risen Jesus only in the Gospel of Matthew.[8]

The testimony of Jesus' sisters would have had an even greater impact upon the brothers of Jesus than it did on the disciples. As social anthropologists have noted, in the society of Jesus' time brother-sister ties were intense and their affection for each other was strong.[9]

A hint of what may have happened to produce the brothers' change of attitude can be found in a fragment of the second-century BCE *Gospel of the Hebrews*. In this apocryphal gospel James the Lord's brother abstains from eating bread until he has a vision of the risen Jesus who says: "the Son of Man is risen from among them that sleep."[10] Although *Gospel of the Hebrews* is chiefly concerned with establishing the primacy of James among those who witnessed the risen Christ, it may nonetheless preserve a genuine tradition that, after hearing of the accounts of his sisters and in the face of other accounts from the disciples of seeing the risen Jesus, James embarked on a fast until he too had a vision.

EARLY LEADERSHIP IN THE JERUSALEM CHURCH

While it is clear that by Pentecost the brothers of Jesus were now among his followers, at this point the movement was under the leadership of the disciple Peter. The early chapters of Acts relate how Peter and his fellow disciple John taught and preached in the temple, healed the sick, got arrested by the temple authorities at least once and possibly twice, and were beaten, imprisoned, and charged not to speak in the name of Jesus. In one story a married couple who have held back money from the sale of

---

7. Mark 15:40; 16:1.
8. Luke 24:4, 10; Matt 28:1, 9–10.
9. Malina, *New Testament World*, 128, 142.
10. See Painter, *Just James*, 185, for the quote from the *Gospel of the Hebrews*.

land are confronted by Peter, and fall down dead.[11] There is no mention of James the Lord's brother in these early stories in Acts.

About three years later, by some scholarly estimates,[12] a Greek-speaking Jewish Christian named Stephen was stoned to death by a mob in Jerusalem, and a persecution began against the Jerusalem Christians, or at least against the Greek-speaking among them. Many Greek-speaking (or Hellenist) Jewish Christians left the city for other parts of Judea and for Samaria.[13] Acts 8:14 then relates, "Now when the apostles at Jerusalem heard that Samaria had accepted the word of God, they sent Peter and John to them." If this text is correct, "the apostles" had authority to send Peter. It would seem that, by this time, a shift in leadership had taken place.

As Lynn P. Eldershaw writes, "The death of the charismatic founding leader has long been identified as a time of instability in a new religious movement, having the potential to provoke disruption, factionalism, dispersal, or even the collapse of a movement."[14] In many religious movements coping with the loss of a charismatic leader, as in many family businesses that have similar succession problems upon the death or retirement of the founder, there is often a division between the close associates of the original leader/founder on the one hand and the family of that individual on the other. Here are three examples of such successions and their outcomes.

LEADERSHIP SUCCESSION: THE LATTER DAY SAINT EXAMPLE

When Joseph Smith, the founder of the Church of Jesus Christ of the Latter Day Saints (LDS, or Mormons),[15] was murdered in Carthage, Illinois, in June, 1844, his designated successors included two of his brothers, who died with or shortly after him, his twelve-year-old son, and an earlier associate who was no longer part of the leadership council. Thus authority at the LDS settlement at Nauvoo, Illinois, passed to the church leadership council known as the Quorum of Twelve. The president of this Quorum

---

11. Acts 5:1–11.
12. See, for example, Hengel, *Acts*, 137.
13. Acts 8:1.
14. Eldershaw, "Collective Identity," 72.
15. Material on the Latter Day Saint movements is summarized from Shields, "Latter Day Saint Movement," 59–78.

of Twelve, Brigham Young, assumed the presidency of the church in the following year but did not claim a prophetic role equivalent to Smith's. Nonetheless he soon initiated doctrines and practices that alienated many of Smith's original followers.

Doctrinal differences involving Young's policies and practices soon caused fragmentation of the original movement. While the largest fraction of believers followed Brigham Young and the Twelve—both figuratively and literally, moving westward to Utah—in the next twenty-five years at least twenty-five offshoots of the original LDS church started up, almost all short-lived. In 1860 the leaders of one of these offshoots, in their search for a prophetic successor to Joseph Smith, formed the Reformed Latter Day Saint Church under the prophetic leadership of Joseph Smith's son, Joseph Smith III. This church remains to the current day the second-largest of the Latter Day Saint denominations.

LEADERSHIP SUCCESSION: THE SHAMBHALA INTERNATIONAL EXAMPLE

Shambhala International,[16] a movement within Tibetan-based Buddhism, was founded by Chögyam Trungpa Rinpoche in 1971. "Rinpoche" was an honorific title for a high-ranking reincarnated Tibetan Buddhist teacher. Trungpa fled Tibet in 1959 and lived in India and England before he and his British wife settled in the United States in 1970 to teach Buddhism to the West. His movement spread rapidly in the 1970s and 1980s until his sudden death in Nova Scotia in 1987. This left the movement in the hands of his Vice President and designated successor.

Less than two years later it became known that this new leader had contracted AIDS and had caused two other people to become infected. With the ensuing notoriety and negative publicity the movement functionally came to a halt and its legal entity was dissolved. By March of 1995, however, a consortium of Trungpa's senior students and other Buddhist authorities appointed Trungpa's eldest son to be the new leader of the movement. Although he was not a strong leader in his early years, the fact that another respected Buddhist leader had a revelation that Trungpa's son was the reincarnation of an earlier respected Buddhist teacher "provided

---

16. Material on Shambhala International is summarized from Eldershaw, "Collective Identity," 72–102.

the necessary validation of his claim to spiritual authority."[17] The movement, under its new leader and with a new name, began once more to flourish.

LEADERSHIP SUCCESSION: THE EARLY ISLAM EXAMPLE

At the death of the Prophet Mohammed in 632 fierce debate erupted over the succession.[18] This threatened to tear the movement apart. Umar ibn al-Khattab, one of the most powerful of the close circle of Mohammed's supporters and advisors who were known as the Companions of the Prophet, then threw his support to another Companion and close advisor, Abu Bakr. Abu Bakr became the leader of the followers of Mohammed and adopted the title *khalifa* or caliph, meaning representative or deputy. Both Umar and Abu Bakr had daughters who had been married to Mohammed, relationships that increased these men's standing among the followers. By a combination of diplomacy and warfare, Abu Bakr regained the support of outlying Arab tribes that had broken off their allegiance at the death of Mohammed. At Abu Bakr's death two years later Umar became the second caliph and continued the movement's military expansion. Umar was assassinated by a Persian slave in 644, but on his deathbed he called for the creation of a council to select his successor.

The council chose a son-in-law of Mohammed's, Uthman ibn Affan, as the third caliph. Uthman was of a different clan than Mohammed, and his appointment of his own clansmen to key positions opened up the question of whether status in Islamic society should depend on one's family and tribal ties or on one's commitment to the Prophet's teachings and the needs of the Islamic community. Resentment of Uthman's nepotism led to his assassination in 656.

His successor was the Prophet's cousin, Ali ibn Ali Talib, who was also Mohammed's son-in-law. Ali's followers regarded him as Mohammed's legitimate successor, but his claim to leadership was disputed by Uthman's kinsmen and two former Companions of the Prophet, Talha ibn Ubayd Allah and al-Zubayr ibn al-Awwam. These two men had the support of one of Mohammed's widows, A'isha, daughter of Abu Bakr. In the Battle of the Camel Ali defeated and killed the former Companions and

---

17. Eldershaw, "Collective Identity," 84.

18. Material on early Islam is summarized from Gordon, *Rise of Islam*, xxx, 11, 16–17, 24–25, 30–31, 33–35, 39–40.

captured Aʾisha. However, he was assassinated by a member of another splinter group in 661.

Uthman's kinsman Muʿawiya I succeeded Ali as caliph and instituted hereditary succession, instead of choice by council, but he faced continued opposition from Ali's son al-Hasan. The followers of Ali and his sons developed into the Shiʿa branch of Islam, while the followers of the caliphs of Muʿawiya's line became the forerunners of Sunni Islam.

LEADERSHIP SUCCESSION: A SUMMARY

In each of the above three examples, the close associates of the deceased leader played somewhat different roles. Only in the case of the Shambhala Buddhists was there an acceptable designated successor, a non-relative, in place upon the death of the charismatic founder. In the LDS and the Islamic movements the leadership group, either the Quorum of Twelve or the Companions of the Prophet, likewise bypassed relatives of the founder and choose a successor from among themselves. In none of these cases was the initial solution to the leadership succession completely satisfactory. In the Shambhala case the designated successor proved unworthy and eventually died of AIDS. In the LDS case, implementation of certain policies by the elected successor (Brigham Young) alienated many of the original followers and provoked extreme fragmentation of the movement. In Islam, the deaths of Abu Bakr and Umar led to a successor who provoked clan and tribal rivalries.

Due to these problems, subsequent solutions to leadership in all three of the above examples involved relatives of the original founder. In the Shambhala movement, students and teachers, the equivalent to companions of the founder in the other two movements, chose the founder's son and supported him through his early less than successful years until he had achieved sufficient prophetic authority. In the other two examples there was a permanent division between those who remained loyal to leaders from the original leadership group (the Quorum of Twelve or the Companions of the Prophet), and those whose loyalty shifted to a relative of the founder (Joseph Smith III or Ali ibn Ali Talib). In the latter two examples, these divisions remained permanent.

LEADERSHIP SUCCESSION: THE JERUSALEM CHURCH

As in the above examples, the first leader of the early Jerusalem believers was one of the associates of the founder, in this case Peter, Jesus' closest disciple. It is most likely that Peter's leadership was that of *primus inter pares*, for Jesus did not designate a successor. Successors in new religious movements usually do not don the mantle of the charismatic leader but most often assume a deputy role, at least nominally, as did Brigham Young and the early caliphs. According to the late second–early third-century CE church father Clement of Alexandria, quoted in Eusebius, after the ascension of Jesus, Peter, James, and John chose James the Just, that is, James the Lord's brother, as the first Bishop of Jerusalem.[19] Eusebius put this appointment after the death of Stephen, although the quote from Clement only says "after the ascension [of Jesus]."

There is no doubt that the death of Stephen and the persecution of the Greek-speaking Christians in Jerusalem was a crisis point in the fledgling movement. It could have provoked the three principal disciples, Peter, James, and John, spontaneously to choose James the Lord's brother as the movement's new leader, but I believe other factors played a decisive role in this change.

One factor that made the succession in the Jerusalem church different from the three examples cited above is that Jesus left a good many adult male relatives behind him: his four brothers, Joseph's brothers Clopas and Judas the son of James, and Joseph's nephews the sons of Alphaeus. These relatives merited a special name in early Christian literature; they were called the *desposynoi*, "those who belong to the master."[20] These kinsmen, who included a sizeable portion of Jesus' original twelve disciples, probably soon pressed for the choice of James the Lord's brother to head the Christian community because James was Jesus' closest male relative and, as the oldest surviving brother, stood next in line in dynastic succession. Later, after James's death, the *desposynoi* played a key role in the choice of the next head of the Jerusalem church, Simon or Simeon the son of Clopas.[21] This Simon was not only the cousin of James on his father's side, but a nephew of Jesus on his mother's side.

---

19. Eusebius, *Hist. Eccl.* 2:1:2–3.
20. Bauckham, *Jude*, 60–63.
21. Ibid., 85–88.

Kinship and genealogy were key factors in the choice of leaders in other Palestinian Jewish religious groups in this era.[22] In a similar situation early in the following century, the choice between two candidates for president of the rabbinic academy at Jamnia was made solely on the basis of genealogy—the chosen candidate was a tenth-generation descendant of Ezra.[23]

JESUS' MOTHER AND SISTERS AS HIS DISCIPLES AND THEIR ROLE IN THE EARLY CHURCH

Another important factor may have been the actions of Jesus' mother and sisters. A study of women in the succession in family-owned businesses, at least those of Asian origin in a cultural milieu where the family was considered more important than the individual, showed that the mothers played the role of buffers or mediators.[24] In early Islam, the Prophet's wife A'isha also attempted to play the role of mediator, although she was unsuccessful.

In recent decades there has been a considerable interest and a great many books written about the role of Mary Magdalene as Jesus' principal female disciple. Most of these works are based on references to a Mary in passages from gnostic works written starting in the second century, when Gnosticism developed as an alternative form of Christianity, one that dealt with mystical knowledge or gnosis. This gnostic Mary is found most notably in the *Gospel of Thomas* and the *Gospel of Mary* but also in later works such as *The Dialogue of the Savior* and the *Pistis Sophia*.

Stephen J. Shoemaker has suggested that this gnostic Mary is a composite figure composed of Mary of Nazareth (Jesus' mother) and Mary Magdalene.[25] He cites the third-century gnostic work *The Gospel of Philip* in which three Marys are mentioned: Mary Magdalene, the mother of Jesus, and the sister of Jesus and suggests that these three women became blurred in gnostic tradition. The only problem with this otherwise useful analysis is that Shoemaker ignores the third Mary, Jesus' sister. I think it likely that Mary, Jesus' sister, disappeared early as a separate individual from most Christian traditions because of the cult of the perpetual

---

22. Bernheim, *James*, 217.
23. Johnson, *Genealogies*, 92, 94.
24. Janjuha-Jivraj, "Impact of the Mother," 781–97.
25. Shoemaker, "Rethinking," 555–95.

virginity of her mother. Whatever role she played as a disciple and figure of importance in the early church would have soon been attached to her mother's identity, particularly because they shared the same name and also because they probably worked together toward a common goal.

In the *Gospel of Mary* the disciple Peter says that the disciples know the Savior loved Mary more than any other woman. Peter and his brother Andrew doubt her vision, however, and at this point she is defended by Levi who says: "If the Savior made her worthy, who are you to reject her? Surely the Savior knows her well. That is why he has loved her more than us."[26]

Now why should Mary be defended by Levi of all people? Levi is not mentioned elsewhere in this work or in similar apocryphal works. As mentioned in chapter 1, when something is illogical or out of place in a story it often stems from an original account. As we also saw in chapter 1, Levi was the cousin of Jesus' sister Mary; thus it makes perfectly good sense for Levi to be defending his cousin, less so for him to be defending his uncle's widow, and none whatsoever for him to be defending Mary Magdalene.

There is another link between a Mary and one of Jesus' close relatives. The early Christian leader Hippolytus, who lived from about 179 to 236, wrote that a gnostic Jewish sect known as the Naassenes venerated James the Lord's brother and attributed to him certain secret teachings transmitted via Mariamne.[27] It is more reasonable to assume that this Mariamne is James's sister or mother than that she is Mary Magdalene.

In the *Gospel of Philip*, Mary the mother of Jesus is described as "a great anathema to the Hebrews, who are the apostles and the apostolic men," an image that, as Shoemaker notes, resonates with conflicts between Mary and Peter found in other gnostic texts.[28]

In the *Gospel of Thomas* Peter says: "Let Mary leave us, for women are not worthy of life," and Jesus replies: "I myself shall lead her in order to make her male, so that she too may become a living spirit resembling you males. For every woman who will make herself male will enter the kingdom of heaven."[29] The *Dialogue with the Savior* does not contain Peter and likewise does not contain a clash between Mary and the named disciples,

---

26. Gos. Mary 18; see Meyer and de Boer, *Gospels of Mary*, 22.
27. See Painter, *Just James*, 5, 174.
28. Gos. Phil. 55:29–30 (NHC II, 3); see Shoemaker, "Rethinking," 572.
29. Gos. Thom. 114 (NHC II, 2); see Robinson et al., *Nag Hammadi Library*, 130.

Judas and Matthew. In the *Pistis Sophia* Mary is praised by Jesus as "one whose heart is set on heaven's kingdom more than all your brothers."[30] Peter goes on to complain about her: "My master, we cannot endure this woman who gets in our way and does not let any of us speak, though she talks all the time."[31] Later in that work Mary expresses her fear of Peter but is vindicated by Jesus.

In all of these works Mary appears as the disciple who understands Jesus better than his male disciples and is praised by Jesus as an exemplar of faith and understanding. This Mary is said to have been beloved of Jesus and is connected to James and Levi, Jesus' close relatives. She appears in some apocryphal works with Salome, Martha, and Mary the mother of Jesus. The case for this Mary being Jesus' sister, or his mother, or in some works a composite of the two women, is far stronger than for her being Mary Magdalene who (outside of the Gospels) is mentioned by name beginning only in the fourth century. It is also worth noting that the esteemed position of Mary the mother of Jesus in the early church probably predated efforts to portray her as a perpetual virgin. This esteemed position may have been, at least in part, due to her descent from high priests, a factor of great importance to Jews in a Jewish congregation of the earlier first century.

Jesus' other sister Salome is found in the New Testament only in the final two chapters of the Gospel of Mark. However, a Salome appears as one of Jesus' disciples in several apocryphal works deriving from Egyptian and eastern Syrian traditions.[32] In four of these works she is an interlocutor, that is, she asks questions of Jesus. While far less prominent than the disciple Mary in these works, she is the secondmost prominent interlocutor, after Mary. Interestingly, in one of the Manichaean *Psalms of Thomas* (the Manichaeans were a sect that started in the third century and were derived partly from Christian roots), Salome builds a tower upon a rock.[33] Thus in this psalm Salome is associated with a rock rather than is the disciple Peter, who is named the rock by Jesus in the Gospel of Matthew.[34]

---

30. *Pistis Soph.* 17; see Meyer and de Boer, *Gospels of Mary*, 66.
31. *Pistis Soph.* 36; see ibid., 68.
32. Bauckham, *Gospel Women*, 237–43.
33. *Psalm of Thomas* 16; see ibid., 255.
34. Matt 16:18; see Corley, "Salome," 88.

In nearly all the apocryphal works noted above a Mary comes into conflict with the disciple Peter, and in the *Psalm of Thomas 16* there is an implied replacement of Peter by Salome. I think these traditions reflect back to the actual situation in the earliest church, when the women in Jesus' family, particularly Mary and her daughter Mary, sought to influence the movement's leadership and thereby came into conflict with Peter. Their influence, especially that of Mary Jesus' mother as the descendant of Jewish high priests and as the mother of Jesus, combined with pressure from Jesus' male relatives in a society where the dynastic principle was so important, caused the leading disciples—Peter and James and John (the sons of Zebedee)—to appoint James the Lord's brother to head the early Christian movement.

JAMES AS LEADER OF THE JERUSALEM CHURCH

At least at first, Peter retained an important role in the movement's leadership. In 1 Pet 5:1 he is referred to (or refers to himself) as the "co-elder." When the Apostle Paul first visited Jerusalem after his conversion, he stayed with Peter for fifteen days and saw none of the other apostles except for James the Lord's brother.[35] This was probably about 36 CE. Early stories in Acts describe Peter's missionary activities in Judea and Samaria.[36] In one story Peter has a vision from God commanding him to eat unclean food forbidden by Jewish law. Immediately after his vision he journeys to the Hellenistic city of Caesarea and baptizes the Roman centurion Cornelius and his household, but Cornelius does not undergo the Jewish rite of circumcision.[37] Once back in Jerusalem Peter meets with criticism from "the circumcision party" because he ate with Cornelius and his household.[38] The issue of whether circumcised Jews should eat with uncircumcised Gentile Christians gained in importance in later years, but this story is the first to highlight the faction of Judaizers within the Jerusalem church with whom James sided, at least to some extent. Representatives of this party, said to have come from James, visited Christians in Antioch and Galatia, urging the full practice of Jewish law and circumcision for male Gentile

---

35. Gal 1:18–19.
36. Acts 8:14–25; 9:32–43.
37. Acts 10.
38. Acts 11:2–18.

converts. Eventually dissent about this issue led to its being brought before a church council in Jerusalem in about 49 CE.[39]

Sometime during these years a body of twelve elders was constituted under the leadership of James, the Lord's brother.[40] These elders became more powerful as Jesus' original twelve disciples left Jerusalem to serve as missionaries, were executed for preaching the new faith, or died of natural causes. In the church council of 49 CE the apostles and elders functioned as an advisory group, but decision-making authority was in the hands of James. When the Apostle Paul returned to Jerusalem in the late 50s he made his report to James and all the elders. It is unclear whether the advice then given to Paul was from James and the elders acting in concert or from the elders alone,[41] but this advice was for Paul to embark on a ritual of Jewish purification. Perhaps not accidently, this advice nearly got Paul killed.

JAMES'S DEATH IN JERUSALEM

There are two accounts of James's death in 62 CE. Josephus records that, in the absence of a Roman governor (the previous one had died in office and the next one was in transit), the high priest Ananus brought James before the Jewish high council, the Sanhedrin, and accused him and some of his companions of being breakers of the law. James and the others were then stoned.[42] Eusebius, quoting Hegesippus, relates that James was brought to the top of the temple in Jerusalem to tell the people gathered there for the Passover that Jesus was not the Messiah. Instead, James referred to the Son of Man title for Jesus and suggested Jesus would come on the clouds of heaven. Because of this statement James was thrown off the parapet of the temple, stoned, and finally clubbed to death.[43]

What is significant in Hegesippus's account is that the people, upon hearing James's testimony, cried "Hosanna to the Son of David." Presumably they are referring to James. As a descendant of David, James had inherited the prestige and the messianic expectation that accompanied his descent—and the danger that went with it. The whole story of his

---

39. Gal 2:12; 5:12–13; Acts 15:1–29.
40. Bauckham, *Jude*, 73–75.
41. Acts 21:23–25.
42. Josephus, *Ant.* 20:200.
43. Eusebius, *Eccl. Hist.* 2:23:1–17.

accusation and execution is infused with Davidic messianic expectations, expectatons that were rising at that time in Palestine, as well as a reaction to those expectations. The high priest Ananus who engineered James's execution was a son of the earlier high priest Ananus (or Annas) who had pressed for the execution of Jesus in 30 CE. It is likely that, as several scholars have noted, *all* executions of early Christians were carried out under Ananide high priests.[44]

The house of Ananus would have had a particular dread of those claiming messianic authority through their descent from David. As noted earlier, one of the most important messianic proof-texts was Num 24:17, which says that the star or scepter shall "break down all the sons of Seth (or Sheth)."[45] This particular prophetic passage is featured in two Dead Sea Scroll documents, one of them arguably the most important in that entire collection, the *Damascus Rule*, where it is quoted as "sons of Seth."[46] The first high priest Ananus (Annas in the Gospels) who with Caiaphas sent Jesus to the Romans for crucifixion was literally a son of Seth,[47] and his descendants would also have been known as the "sons of Seth" in popular parlance. This connection would have been common knowledge amongst Palestinian Jews. Ananus son of Seth and his five sons, who all became high priests, would have known of it and responded accordingly to anyone who might claim messianic authority, particularly any descendants of David such as Jesus or James.

---

44. Crossan, *Birth of Christianity*, 509; Kokkinos, *Dynasty*, 383; VanderKam, *Joshua*, 478.

45. It is translated as "territory of all the Shethites" in the NRSV.

46. Damascus Rule (CD 7:21). This phrase is also in 4Q175:13 as "sons of Sheth." See Vermes, *Complete Dead Sea Scrolls*, 133, 496.

47. VanderKam, *Joshua*, 420–21.

4

Peter and Mark in Rome

IN 39 OR 40 CE the Roman Emperor Gaius Caligula (his second name means "Little Boot") decreed that a statue of himself in the guise of the god Jupiter be placed in the Jewish temple in Jerusalem. There was outrage among the Jews of Judea and Galilee, a Jewish embassy went to the emperor in Rome, Roman troops were sent to Galilee, and there was the real possibility of war in Palestine.[1] The crisis was resolved only by Caligula's death in January 41 CE and the accession of the Emperor Claudius to the imperial throne.

One result of this change in emperors was a grant by Claudius to a grandson of King Herod's, Herod Agrippa I, to rule the territories of Judea and Samaria as a client king. Agrippa I (as he was usually known) had previously been ruling Galilee and Peraea and some smaller territories, and now he had control of nearly all of Palestine. According to the book of Acts, Agrippa I executed the disciple James the son of Zebedee and arrested the disciple Peter. Only through the intervention of an angel was Peter miraculously released from prison, after which he went to the house of Mary the mother of John Mark. After telling the Christians gathered in the house to notify James the Lord's brother and the brethren of his release, Peter "departed and went to another place."[2]

One early second-century Christian writer, Papias, is quoted in much later sources as saying that John the son of Zebedee was also a martyr.[3] Another indication of this John's martyrdom is found in the Gospel of Mark, in which Jesus says to the two brothers, "The cup that I drink you will drink; and the baptism with which I am baptized, you will be

---

1. Theissen, *Gospels*, 125–65; Taylor, "Palestinian Christianity and the Caligula Crisis. Part I," 101.

2. Acts 12:1–17 (quote from verse 17).

3. Hengel, *Johannine Question*, 21, 158 n. 121; see also Culpepper, *John*, 170–74; Boismard, *Martyre de Jean*.

baptized."[4] Since Jesus was speaking of his own martyrdom, he must also have been speaking of the martyrdom of both James and John. But with another early Christian tradition—that John had lived to be an old man and died in Ephesus—it is possible that the name of John brother of James was removed at a very early time from the original passage in Acts.

Peter's whereabouts after he fled Jerusalem is uncertain, but Eusebius in his *History of the Church* says that about this time Peter went to Rome to combat the magician Simon Magnus, and a Latin version of Eusebius's *Chronicle* puts Peter's arrival in the second year of the Emperor Claudius.[5] The apocryphal second-century work the *Acts of Peter* recounts a whole series of duels between the two miracle-workers, Simon Magnus and Peter, with Peter winning.[6] According to the fourth-century church father Jerome, Peter arrived in Rome in 42 CE.[7] The only other early text that may support Peter's arrival in Rome at this time is a note preserved by Augustine that the "law of the Jews" (possibly a reference to the first Christian teaching since a large Jewish community already existed in Rome) came from Syria to Rome during or shortly after the reign of Caligula.[8] According to the third-century Roman historian Dio Cassius, the Jews of Rome rioted in the first year of the Emperor Claudius, resulting in a prohibition of their meetings, but Dio Cassius makes a point of saying the Jews were not expelled at this time.[9] There is no direct mention of Peter or of Christians in either of these entries, however. The account in Acts and Paul's letter to the Galatians show that Peter was in Antioch and Jerusalem in the late 40s. Nonetheless Paul's first letter to the Corinthians does point out that Peter and his wife traveled together and probably had visited the Christian community in Corinth.[10]

Also in Corinth by about 51 CE were Aquila and Priscilla, who according to Acts 18:2 were among the Jews recently evicted from Rome by the Emperor Claudius. According to the Roman historian Suetonius, Claudius expelled the Jews of Rome sometime in his reign, perhaps in the

4. Mark 10:39.

5. Eusebius, *Eccl. Hist.* 2:14; 2:15:2; 2:17:1; for mention in Eusebius's *Chronicle*, see Crossley, *Date of Mark's Gospel*, 11.

6. Ehrman, *Lost Scriptures*, 135–54.

7. Jerome, *On Illustrious Men*, 5.

8. Hengel, *Acts*, 108.

9. For Dio Cassius, *Hist.* 6:6 see Taylor, "Popular Opposition," 55 n. 1.

10. 1 Cor 1:12; 9:5.

year 49, because of "disturbances caused by Chrestus among the Jews of Rome."[11] Although there has been much debate by scholars on this issue, the preponderance of the information available suggests that Chrestos is a corrupt form of the word Christos, and that these disturbances were occasioned by conflict between traditional Jews and those who became followers of Christ.[12] Some scholars have suggested that this imperial edict expelling Jews was the same as the one forbidding their meetings in the year 41 CE, but H. Dixon Slingerland has pointed out how irreconcilable the two accounts really are.[13] Also, one wonders if the Jewish Christian presence in Rome in 41 CE would have been large enough to merit such a disturbance. Later in the decade, and after missionary work by the disciple Peter, these Christians could have reached a critical mass, numerous enough to have caused significant friction within the Roman Jewish community and to merit imperial and historical attention.

According to Christian tradition as early as the late first century, Peter and Paul both died in Rome as the result of persecution by the Emperor Nero.[14] The Roman historian Tacitus wrote that Nero put the blame of Rome's disastrous fire of July, 64 CE onto the Christians and executed a good many of them.[15]

1 PETER

There is one New Testament letter purported to have been written by Peter from Rome, 1 Peter. Most scholars regard this work as pseudonymous despite the statement in the letter's first verse that the letter is from "Peter,

---

11. Suetonius, *Claud.* 25:4, mentions the expulsion; see Hengel, *Acts*, 108. However the date, 49, is quoted only from a spurious or nonextant version of Josephus; see Schwartz, *Agrippa I*, 94 n. 20.

12. The suggestion that Chrestus was a Jewish activist living in Rome is negated by the fact that "the name of Chrestus does not appear among the several hundred known names of Roman Jews" (Leon, *Jews of Ancient Rome*, 25 n. 2). The more recent idea that Chrestus was an associate of the Emperor Claudius is negated by the fact that after a thorough search no such Chrestus has been identified (Slingerland, *Claudian Policymaking*, 201). These facts, combined with the fact that Taciticus (*Ann.* 15:44) uses the term "chrestianus" instead of "christianus" to refer to Christians, support the interpretation that the name Chrestus in Suetonius *Claud.* 25:4 is actually Christus, and a reference to Jesus.

13. For those who wish to harmonize the two accounts see Slingerland, "Seutonius *Claudius 25.4* and the Account in Cassius Dio," 306 n. 4. For the conclusion that the two accounts are irreconcilable see ibid., 305–22.

14. Eusebius, *Eccl. Hist.* 2:25.

15. Tacitus, *Ann.* 15:44; see Black, *Mark*, 228–29.

an Apostle of Jesus Christ." Two recent studies of 1 Peter give virtually the same reasons for this conclusion:[16]

1) Its polished Attic Greek, Classical vocabulary, and evidence of Classical rhetorical training make it unlikely that it was written by Peter.
2) The Old Testament quotations are from the Greek-language version of the Hebrew Bible, the Septuagint, rather than from the Hebrew scriptures themselves. In fact, the writer shows a clear familiarity with the Septuagint.
3) There is no mention of Jesus' or Peter's experiences.
4) There is no evidence that Peter ever went on a missionary journey to northern Asia Minor, where the recipients of this letter are stated to be. In fact, there is little evidence of any Christian churches in these provinces during Peter's lifetime.
5) There is no mention of Paul, who would have been in Rome with Peter in the early 60s CE.
6) The reference to Babylon at the end of the letter, clearly a reference to Rome, indicates a date after Peter's death, for Babylon as Rome appears in Jewish literature written after the conquest of Judea and destruction of the Temple in 70 CE,[17] and Peter is thought to have been killed during the persecutions by the Emperor Nero in the mid-60s CE.[18]

Pseudonymity presents its own set of problems, however. Contrary to earlier scholarly assumptions, pseudonymous letters in the ancient world and in the early church were condemned as forgeries.[19] As Karen H. Jobes notes: "Pseudonymity appears to have been an acceptable literary device when the alleged author had been dead for centuries, as in the case of Enoch and Solomon. However, when generated relatively soon after the alleged author's death (or during his lifetime as in the case of Galen!), it appears to have been viewed as a forgery and rejected when its true origin was discovered."[20]

16. Elliott, *1 Peter*, 120–21; Senior, "1 Peter," 4.
17. Hunzinger, "Babylon," 67–77.
18. Eusebius, *Eccl. Hist.* 2:25.
19. Metzger, "Literary Forgeries," 6, 12–14; Ehrman, *Lost Christianities*, 30–31.
20. Jobes, *1 Peter*, 16.

Jobes goes on to note that if the inclusion of Sylvanus as the bearer in 1 Peter 5:12 was a fictional device to give the letter verisimilitude, it could not have been actually delivered to its stated recipients but must have been written by someone who presented it as a long-lost letter that had been rediscovered.[21] However, John Elliott presents several solid reasons why 1 Peter was not written after about 92 CE, most notably that the letter contains no reference to defections from the faith mentioned by Pliny the Younger to have occurred at about that time in Pontis or to the death of martyrs that occurred about 95 CE in Asia.[22] Elliott also points out that the imminent expectation of the return of Christ, the lack of reference to any church structure, and the total lack of concern with internal heresies or Gnosticism suggests 1 Peter was written earlier than the late first century.

David Meade attempted to circumvent some of the problems of pseudonymity by suggesting that 1 Peter was written shortly after Peter's death to encourage his surviving communities in Asia Minor.[23] If this were the case, then Sylvanus and Mark would have to have been real people known to the recipients of the letter. Meade also noted (see item 6 above) that "the identification of Rome with Babylon need not depend on the destruction of the temple. Already in Daniel, 'Babylon' has become an eschatological symbol of a world power (1:1–8; 3:8–12; 6:2–24). In Revelation (14:8; 17:5, 18; 18:2) it is used of Rome in reference to the persecution of the saints, not the destruction of Jerusalem. *Thus there is nothing to prevent the rise of its usage in Christian apocalyptic circles before AD 70* [my italics]."[24]

A NEW HYPOTHESIS ON THE ORIGIN OF 1 PETER

Karen H. Jobes has offered a new hypothesis for the time, setting, purpose, and recipients of 1 Peter.[25] Rather than being written in the 60s or later, she hypothesizes that it was written in Rome in the early 50s, between Paul's first and third missionary journeys. This would explain

---

21. Ibid., 321.

22. Elliott, *1 Peter*, 135–36; idem, "Roman Provenance of 1 Peter," 186 n. 5; see also Achtemeier, *1 Peter*, 48, 49–50.

23. Meade, *Pseudonymity and Canon*, 172.

24. Ibid., 165.

25. Jobes, *1 Peter*, 19–44.

why the letter does not address regions visited by Paul on his first journey but does include some areas that would become part of Paul's mission area in the course of his third journey. It is also why the letter makes no mention of Paul himself, who wrote his New Testament letter to the Romans at a later date and did not get to Rome until the end of that decade (see item 5, above). She hypothesizes that the recipients of 1 Peter were Roman Christians, possibly both Gentile and Jewish, who had been expelled from Rome by the edict of the Emperor Claudius in the late 40s and displaced to new Claudian colonies in the provinces mentioned in the letter. Jobes notes that coins and ancient texts confirm that Claudius established a *colonia* or colony in each and every one of the provinces named in 1 Peter 1:1 (see figure 3).

For the most part, this large area had only a few small cities and a diverse population of indigenous peoples, Greek settlers, and Roman colonists. Newcomers from Rome would be seen as "foreigners" and "resident aliens" as they are so named in 1 Peter.[26] The disciple Peter would have had ties to these early Christians had he previously been in Rome in the 40s. Peter did not address "churches" in 1 Peter because formal churches had not yet developed in these colonies. He was instead concerned to address the problems these Christians were having in their new communities rather than reiterate the teaching of Jesus or his own preaching (see item 3 above).

Jobes's hypothesis solves many of the awkward problems regarding the composition of 1 Peter, including whether or not Peter actually visited these remote areas of Asia Minor (item 4 above). He did not—he wrote to people now living there whom he had met elsewhere, probably in Rome.

To address the objections of the Attic Greek in 1 Peter (item 1, above), Jobes undertakes an analysis of the epistle's syntax, comparing it to that of a work written by a native Greek speaker (Polybius), to Josephus's work (written by a Greek-speaking scribe), and to Hebrews 5–9 and 1 Thessalonians.[27] Although her analysis of 1 Peter clearly shows signs of Semitic interference in the syntax, it also reveals syntactical signs of composition Greek. In fact, 1 Peter shows a more bimodal distribution—composition Greek versus translation Greek—than do any of the other works in her analysis.

---

26. Elliott, *Home for the Homeless*, 24–37.
27. Jobes, *1 Peter*, 325–38.

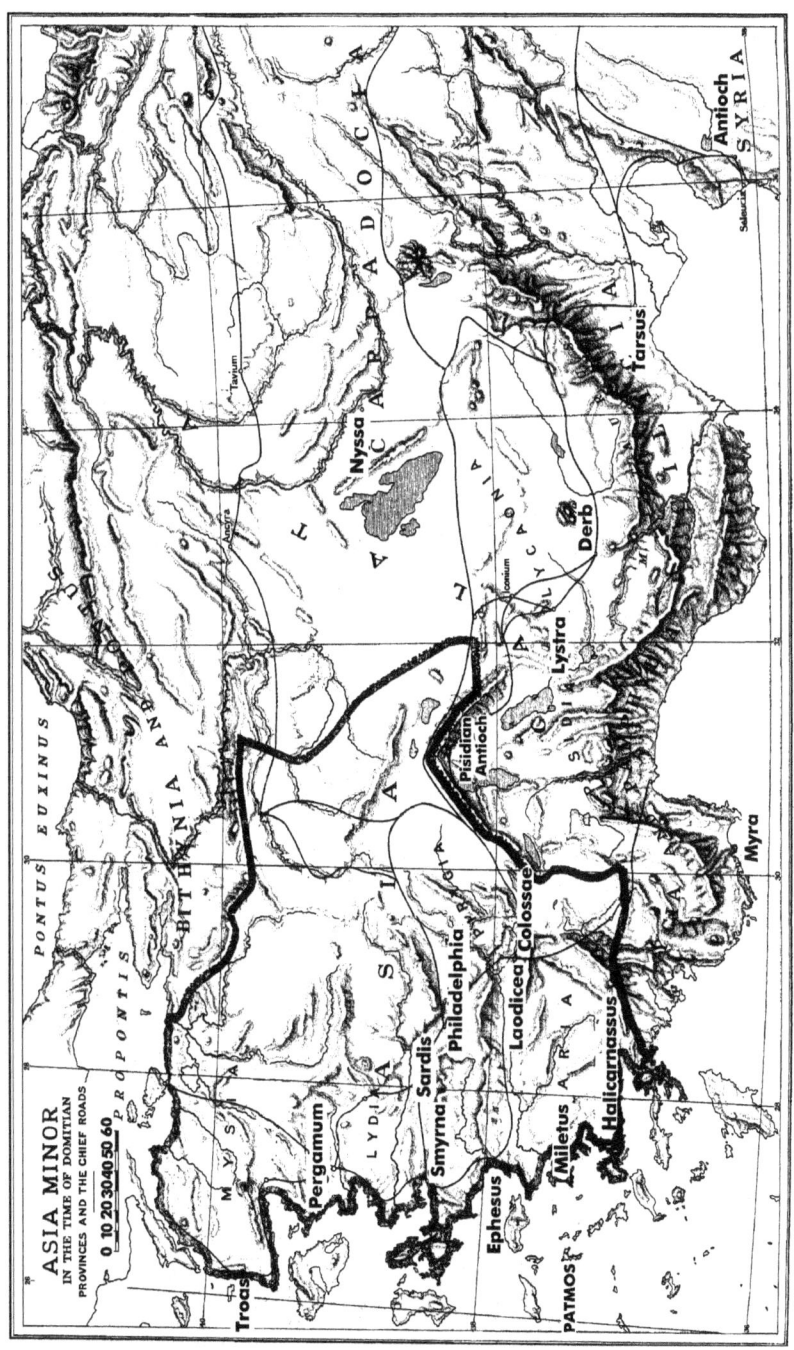

FIGURE 3. Map of Asia Minor in the Late First Century CE. Adapted from Swete, *The Apocalypse of St. John*. Scale is in miles.

This bimodal distribution lends support to the amanuensis hypothesis, that is, that the letter was written by a secretary who was fluent in Greek and familiar with rhetorical and letter-writing conventions.[28] According to this hypothesis, this secretary was Greek-speaking and, whether a Jew or a Gentile "god-fearer," quite familiar with the Septuagint and able to weave its passages into the letter (see item 2, above). The message probably originated in oral Aramaic and progressed either to written Aramaic *or* to an oral translation into Greek, retaining Semitic interference, then to written Greek notes (either a translation of the written Aramaic or a written version of the oral Greek translation), then to the composition of the letter itself. The fact that the writer of the letter retained a clearly detectable amount of Semitic syntactical interference means that she or he was carefully following these notes. Rather than being Silvanus, who was clearly "the bearer" of the letter,[29] the actual writer might have been one of the many scribes or secretaries who copied literary works and wrote letters in ancient Rome.[30] These were usually either slaves or freedmen, and one of them certainly could have been an early Christian. This secretary also could have had the background to introduce a moderate amount of Greek rhetorical style and write in the Attic Greek found in the text of 1 Peter.

The actual writer is important because he or she introduced a peculiar term at the end of 1 Peter, one not found elsewhere in the New Testament: "The co-elect of Babylon greets you, as also Mark, my son."[31] Of recent scholars, only Judith Applegate rejects the consensus that the co-elect refers to the church, a word that does not appear in 1 Peter.[32] Instead, she suggests that the co-elect may refer to a known woman in Asia Minor. Other scholars have objected to her suggestion. Ernest Best argued: "she [the female co-elect] would hardly have been so well-known over so wide an area that such a vague reference would identify her."[33] John Elliott also rejected Applegate's suggestion of a female or wifely co-elect on the grounds that such anonymity is inconsistent with the explicit

---

28. Elliott, *1 Peter*, 123; see also Richards, *Letter Writing*, 59–79, 80–89.
29. Elliott, *1 Peter*, 123–24; Senior, "1 Peter," 5, 152; Jobes, *1 Peter*, 320.
30. McDonnell, "Writing, Copying," 469–91; Haines-Eitzen, *Guardians of Letters*, 23–32.
31. 1 Pet 5:13. The term "co-elect" does not appear in most English translations.
32. Applegate, "Co-elect Woman," 587–604.
33. Best, *1 Peter*, 177.

naming of Silvanus and Mark. Why, Elliott asked, would Peter mention the names of Silvanus and Mark but not that of his own wife?[34]

Perhaps Peter would have mentioned his wife's name, but the actual writer of the text, following Greek writing conventions, would not have. As Mary Rose D'Angelo noted: it was the Greek view that the names of respectable women should not be made public.[35] First Peter was definitely a public letter, intended to be heard by a number of people. Probably the language and style of this letter were intentionally polished to counteract accusations that these early Christians in Asia Minor were following a "barbaric" (defined that is, as non-Greek-speaking) cult. Moreover, Peter's wife (who is mentioned as accompanying her husband in 1 Cor 9:5) would have been known to the displaced members of the Roman Christian community in Asia Minor and would fit very well within the context of Jobes's hypothesis. Using the term co-elect for Peter's wife also fits with the fact that other compounds using "co-" in 1 Peter refer specifically to relationships between husbands and wives.[36] Given the real likelihood that the co-elect mentioned in 1 Pet 5:13 is Peter's wife, the likelihood that the next part of the verse refers to Peter's biological son becomes compelling.

PRESERVATION OF THE MEMORY OF MARK AS PETER'S SON

That the memory of a son of Peter named Mark did not get passed down in the early church is not surprising, for several reasons. First, the most characteristic feature of memory, and thus of tradition dependent upon memory, is *forgetting*. In one typical study of memory retention, 30 percent of one researcher's own life events were forgotten in six months and 71 percent after five years.[37] As information is passed on there is both selectivity and interpretation, as items no longer deemed useful are discarded and others are reinterpreted to meet the current needs of the group. Since early Christians stressed the importance of the family of believers as opposed to one's own relatives,[38] there would have been a strong

---

34. Elliott, *1 Peter*, 881.

35. D'Angelo, "(Re)Presentations of Women in the Gospels: John and Mark," 138 and 147 n. 38.

36. Applegate, "Co-elect Woman," 600.

37. Wagenaar, "My Memory," 232–34.

38. Matt 12:46–50; 19:29; Mark 3:31–35; 10:29–30; Luke 8:19–21; 18:29–30.

incentive for these early Christians not to remember family ties relating to any of the church's founding figures. This is a major reason why we know next to nothing about the families of the apostles and other figures in the early church.

Perhaps most importantly, the knowledge that Mark was Peter's son was a casualty of the "everybody knows" phenomenon: what everybody knows isn't written down because everybody knows it. Elizabeth Weyland Barber and Paul Barber call this the "Silence Principle."[39] As Joel Marcus pointed out, the Second Gospel was originally anonymous because everybody in Mark's original audience knew who the author was.[40] As time passes such information is lost as people die, and eventually no one knows it anymore.

MARK IN THE NEW TESTAMENT

In the New Testament, there are three separate groups of references to someone named Mark. There is "John whose other name was Mark" in the book of Acts.[41] There is "Mark" in the Pauline and pastoral epistles.[42] Finally, there is "Mark my son" in 1 Pet 5:13. Although most scholars consider these as references to the same individual,[43] C. Clifton Black concluded in his extensive examination of Mark that "Mark in the New Testament has emerged as surprisingly complex. Indeed, *it seems that there is not one but at least two, and perhaps three, figures of Mark explicit in the Christian canon* [his italics]."[44]

The first Mark in the New Testament is John Mark. He appears as a rather minor figure, the son of the woman, Mary, who owns a house in Jerusalem to which Peter goes after he has been miraculously delivered from prison.[45] In the next chapter of Acts John Mark goes on a missionary journey with Paul and Barnabas, but leaves in mid-journey. Later, Barnabas and Paul quarrel about taking John Mark on another journey

---

39. Barber and Barber, *When They Severed Earth from Sky*, 17–33.
40. Marcus, *Mark*, 17.
41. Acts 12:12, 25; 13:5, 13; 15:37–39.
42. Phlm 24; Col 4:10; 2 Tim 4:11.
43. Brown, *Introduction*, 159; Elliott, *1 Peter*, 887–88; Jefford, "Mark, John," 557–58; Martin, "Mark, John," 259–60; Senior, "1 Peter," 155.
44. Black, *Mark*, 66.
45. Acts 12:12–17.

because Paul does not want him along and Barnabas does and proceeds to do so.[46] John Mark is clearly cast in a subsidiary role to Paul and Barnabas, but he seems to have some latent importance; otherwise why mention him at all? This importance is not really explained by the supposed relationship to Barnabas,[47] which is not mentioned in Acts. Moreover, as Clifton Black asks, why was John Mark selected, from among all the Jerusalem faithful, to accompany Barnabas and Paul in the first place, to be a servant of the word or eyewitness on their mission?[48]

It is worth noting that the writer of Acts uses the identifier "Mary the mother of John Mark" not to identify John Mark, but to identify *Mary*, to distinguish her from other Marys in the early Jerusalem church. As noted in chapter 1, Mary was one of the two or three most common Jewish women's names in Second Temple times.[49] Jewish women in Second Temple times were usually identified by the name of their father, *not* by the name of their husband(s).[50] For example, the writer of Luke-Acts identifies the prophetess Anna as the daughter Phanuel but not by the name of her husband,[51] although both men were obviously long deceased. This makes a good deal of sense, since a woman can have only one father but, theoretically at least, several husbands.

Like a number of Jewish women named in ossuary inscriptions from Second Temple times, Jewish women in the Synoptic Gospels and Acts are often identified by their son or sons.[52] In addition to Mary the mother of John Mark there is Mary the mother of Jesus, Mary the mother of James the lesser and Joses, and the mother of the sons of Zebedee.[53] This last woman is not described as the wife of Zebedee, although Zebedee is

46. Acts 15:37–39.
47. Col 4:10.
48. Acts 13:5; see Black, *Mark*, 28, 31–33, 35.
49. Hachlili, "Hebrew Names," 87, 115; Ilan, *Lexicon*, 9.
50. Ilan, *Jewish Women*, 55 and n. 35; Hachlili, "Hebrew Names," 86. In looking at inscriptional evidence from Jewish Palestine, Richard Bauckham, "Mary of Clopas," 236, found sixteen inscriptions of women described by reference to their husbands and nineteen (two of whom were married) by reference to their fathers. He concluded that the former usage was more common since "some (perhaps most) of those described as daughters must have been unmarried." However, there is no evidence presented that these women "must have been" unmarried.
51. Luke 2:36–38.
52. For the ossuary evidence see Rahmani, *Catalogue of Jewish Ossuaries*, 15.
53. Acts 12:12; 1:14; Mark 15:40; 16:1; Luke 24:8–11; Matt 20:20; 27:56.

mentioned as being alive.[54] Mary the mother of James the lesser and Joses was also the wife of Clopas, but is referred to as such only in John,[55] a work written to a Greek-speaking, and probably mostly Gentile, audience.[56] The practice in the Synoptic Gospels and Acts of referring to women by the names of their sons rather than their husbands or fathers is the same as the modern Arab custom of identifying a woman or a man *only* by the name of her or his oldest son.[57]

It has been sometimes thought that this Mary's house was the house with the upper room that was the headquarters of the Jerusalem church.[58] However, although "many were gathered together and were praying" at this house, neither James nor any of the brethren—the church leaders, that is—were there, although they were apparently not far away.[59] This indicates that Mary's house was not the church's headquarters. Yet Peter goes first and only to this house after he gets out of prison, an action that suggests that his family lived in this house.

In Gal 1:18 Paul writes of having stayed fifteen days with Peter in Jerusalem. By implication Peter and his family were living somewhere that would accommodate a guest, and that was in some sense "Peter's." In Second Temple times daughters could inherit from their mothers.[60] Peter's wife or his mother-in-law, who owned the house in Capernaum, could have bought the Jerusalem house from her inheritance, or from the sale of her Capernaum house or the family fishing license (see chapter 6), when the family moved from Galilee. The mother-in-law had probably died by this time, ca. 41 CE, leaving the house to her daughter, but under Jewish law Peter would have the use of (usufruct) his wife's house and so could accommodate guests such as Paul.[61] All of these elements point to

---

54. Mark 1:21 and Matt 4:20.

55. John 19:25.

56. For Mary the mother of James the lesser and Joses see Bauckham, "Salome the Sister of Jesus," 248 n. 6, and Sivertsen, "New Testament Genealogies," 46. In referring to Mary of Clopas in John 19:25, Bauckham, "Mary of Clopas," 236, concludes that the Greek idiom in which the relationship is expressed by the genitive alone would probably be more likely to indicate a husband than a father.

57. Segev, *One Palestine, Complete*, 371.

58. Swete, *St. Mark*, xiv–xv.

59. Acts 12:12, 17.

60. Ilan, *Jewish Women*, 16.

61. Wegner, *Chattel or Person?*, 15–16, 33.

the conclusion that Mary the mother of John Mark was Peter's wife and John Mark was Mark, Peter's son.

The fact that John Mark is not specifically identified as Peter's son is because "everybody knew" who he was at the time Acts was written. An additional very real possibility, related to this "everybody knew" aspect, is that the manuscript of Acts was not finished—given its final polishing—before its author died. As W. A. Strange noted: "The roughness of the common text of Acts suggests further that Luke had not given the work his final attention. There are too many obscure and incoherent passages in the book for one to be satisfied that it represents his finished work.[62] And finally, the rather negative and subservient portrayal of John Mark in Acts[63] is another intentional attempt by Luke to downplay the authority and position of Peter's son, much as Luke had done in the first volume of his work (see chapter 6).

In the Fourth Gospel we learn that Simon Peter's father's name was John.[64] In Matthew Jesus calls Peter *Bariōna* (Barjona).[65] As Richard Bauckham points out, rather than meaning son of Jonah, this term is much more likely to be a transliteration of "son of *Yôḥanaʾ*" an Aramaic form of the name John.[66] John was the fifth most popular name amongst Palestinian Jewish men of the time, while Jonah was ranked eightieth.[67] This particular Aramaic form for John may have been used in reference to Peter because with the Aramaic "bar" (son of) it would form a nickname, meaning "brigand" or "ruffian."[68] Simon Peter, after all, carried a sword and was known to use it.[69]

Names for Jewish males in Second Temple times were strongly patrilineal, and as we saw in chapter 1, a son was most likely to be named for the father's father or the father. Thus a son of Simon Peter was most likely to have been named either John or Simon. The name John, whose other name was Mark, fits precisely with this naming pattern, another example of *paponymy*. As Margaret Williams notes, the name Mark was

62. Strange, *Text of Acts*, 186.
63. Acts 13:5, 13; 15:37–39.
64. John 1:42, 21:15, 16.
65. Matt 16:17; see Bauckham, *Eyewitnesses*, 104.
66. Ibid., 104 n. 39.
67. Ibid., 85, 87.
68. Schwartz, *Agrippa I*, 123.
69. John 18:10.

most likely added during travels abroad, being easier for Greek and Latin speakers to cope with than "Yehohanan."[70]

If John Mark was Peter's son, he would have been a good person for Paul and Barnabas to bring with them on their first mission to Cyprus and beyond (described in Acts 13). This would be particularly true if he was one of the few original witnesses to Jesus' earthly ministry who spoke Greek well enough to preach to a Greek-speaking audience.

CONFLATED MARKS IN EARLY CHRISTIAN TRADITION

After the New Testament, the earliest traditional reference to Mark is by Papias, bishop of Hierapolis in western Asia Minor in the early second century, quoted in Eusebius in the early fourth century: "Now this is what the elder used to say: 'Mark became Peter's interpreter and wrote accurately whatever he remembered, but not in order, of the things said or done by the Lord.['] For he had neither heard the Lord, nor had he followed him, but later on, as I said, [followed] Peter, who used to offer the teachings in anecdotal form but not making, as it were, a systematic arrangement of the Lord's oracles, so that Mark did not miss the mark in thus writing down individual items as he remembered them."[71]

The Papias account contains a number of discrepancies with the picture of Mark found in the New Testament. Mark the Pauline friend and coworker (Phln 24) is said to have been a cousin of Barnabas (Col 4:10) who was a native of Cyprus. However, nothing in the Pauline or pastoral epistles links this Mark to Peter, and yet Papias says that Mark was Peter's interpreter.

Because the composite picture of Mark from Acts and the Pauline and pastoral letters and the Mark mentioned in early church tradition does not fit the picture of a son of Peter, the idea that Mark was Peter's son has been rejected by virtually all scholars.[72] However, as Dennis E. Nineham noted, Mark was "the commonest Latin name in the Roman Empire and ... the early church must have contained innumerable Marks."[73] C. Clifton Black suggested that "different figures named Mark could well have been conflated into one legendary composite, later identified with the Second

---

70. Williams, "Palestinian Jewish Personal Names," 105.
71. Eusebius, *Eccl. Hist.* 3:39, quoted in Black, *Mark*, 83.
72. One exception is Haslehurst, "Mark, My Son," 34–36.
73. Nineham, *Saint Mark*, 39; see also Swete, *St. Mark*, xiii–xiv.

Evangelist."[74] This would have been the case whether Mark died in Alexandria in the year 62, as recounted by Jerome, or later.[75]

As Peter's interpreter John Mark may well have accompanied his parents to Rome. As Bruce Malina has noted, "in the first-century world, adult male children usually remained within or close by the parental household."[76] If, as I have suggested, the Semiticisms in the syntax of 1 Peter originated with the Aramaic utterances of Peter, the Apostle would have been in need of an interpreter on his visits to Rome.

---

74. Black, *Mark*, 10.

75. Jerome, *On Illustrious Men*, 8; but see Swete, *St. Mark*, xxvii, who suggests that Jerome may have made an "unsound inference from the Eusebian date for the succession of Annianus" for Mark's death.

76. Malina, *New Testament World*, 126.

5

The Composition of the Gospel of Mark

TRADITIONS ON THE COMPOSITION OF MARK

THE EARLIEST TRADITION CONCERNING the composition of the Gospel of Mark is from the early second-century Christian writer Papias, quoted in the previous chapter. Richard Bauckham has suggested that the verb "accompanied" is a better translation than "followed" in this passage, since the Greek word means "to go closely with." Thus Mark "neither heard the Lord nor accompanied him, but later on, as I said, [accompanied] Peter."[1]

Another tradition, from Titus Flavius Clemens (Clement, ca. 150–215 CE) of Alexandria in Egypt, is that Mark had been urged by the Christians in Rome to write down Peter's preaching as a memorandum (or notes, *hypomnēma*), and that Peter neither actively prevented nor promoted it.[2] Other church traditions about Mark seem ultimately to derive from these two.[3]

A third tradition, from the late second-century bishop Irenaeus of Lyons (ca. 130–200 CE), states that Mark was the disciple and interpreter of Peter and wrote his gospel after the departure or death of Peter and Paul from Rome.[4] This tradition was probably at least partly dependent on Papias and is at odds with that of Clement, since in Clement there is no mention of Paul and by implication, Peter and Mark are still in contact when the Gospel was written—Peter does not leave Rome or die in Clement's tradition. Of the two, Irenaeus versus Clement, Irenaeus is known to have problems with chronology, giving Jesus a ministry of ten

---

1. Bauckham, *Eyewitnesses*, 203.
2. The three comments of Clement on Mark are quoted in Black, *Mark*, 137–39.
3. Black, *Mark*, 170–71, 184; Bauckham, *Eyewitnesses*, 235–38.
4. For Irenaeus, *Haer.* 3:1:1, see Black, *Mark*, 99–100.

years and having him die near the age of fifty.[5] Clement may have the better information, living in the city where Mark was said to have lived.

Many modern scholars have discounted these traditions, particularly that of Papias, in large part because they can see no real connection to the Apostle Peter and the Second Gospel other than the connection between Mark and Peter in 1 Pet 5:13.[6] An important recent work by Richard Bauckham, *Jesus and the Eyewitnesses*, effectively answers these objections, pointing out the remarkable frequency that Peter's name occurs in Mark, the *inclusio* of eyewitness testimony, and the plural-to-singular narrative device that signals the telling by a member of the group in question, that is, the disciples.[7] Bauckham notes that "taken together, these features make Mark a Gospel that presents, to a far larger degree than the others, a Petrine perspective on the story of Jesus."[8] The quote by Papias in particular is an apologetic for Mark's writing style rather than an artificial attempt to connect the Second Gospel to a known Apostle, Peter.

There is another probable mention of Mark in the possibly second-century work known as the Muratorian Canon that says: "among which, however [or nonetheless] he was present, and so he set it down."[9] The text is torn off before the beginning of this quote, so we are left to wonder, Mark was present *where? when?* why "however" or "nonetheless?"

I believe Papias's account and this passage in the Muratorian Canon apply to John Mark Peter's son (and not Mark the Pauline friend, who was another person). For clarity, I will henceforth refer to Peter's son simply as Mark. At the beginning of Jesus' ministry Peter's son was a boy of less than twelve years. In the three years of Jesus' ministry the child Mark did not accompany Jesus and the disciples on journeys through Galilee and adjacent territories, and thus did not hear Jesus preach. At the time of the last journey to Jerusalem, however, Mark had passed into young manhood, bearing in mind that the transition to adulthood is about the age of thirteen for young Jewish males then and now.[10] Mark

---

5. For Irenaeus, *Haer.* 2:22:5, 6, see Crossley, *Date of Mark's Gospel*, 8.

6. See Black, *Mark*, 86–94, for a history of scholarly interpretations of Papias's description of Mark.

7. Bauckham, *Eyewitnesses*, 124–27, 156–64.

8. Ibid., 171.

9. Black, *Mark*, 97; Ehrman, *Lost Scriptures*, 332. For sources defending the second-century date for the Canon see Bauckham, *Eyewitnesses*, 426 n. 35.

10. Kaplan and Joseph, "Bar Mitzvah, Bat Mitzvah, 164."

accompanied his father and the rest of the disciples and many women to Jerusalem for the Passover, which is the reason why this time period takes up such a preponderantly large percentage (about one-third) of the Second Gospel, and why it is the *only* Passover mentioned in this Gospel. Although certainly not a full participant, Mark was "nonetheless" present at the Last Supper and the later events on the Mount of Olives. However, Mark needed to rely on Peter's preaching for nearly all of what Jesus actually spoke and did during his actual ministry. Only when events in the Second Gospel took place in Capernaum itself was Mark an eyewitness during this ministry. This aspect of the Second Gospel will be discussed in the following chapter.

Modern scholars have also suggested that the Gospel of Mark was composed in various places other than Rome: Syria, Galilee, the Decapolis, Hellenistic Palestine, northern TransJordan, and Egypt.[11] Joel Marcus, for example, has suggested a Syrian setting in the aftermath of the Jewish revolt of 66–70 CE but also notes that "most of the exegesis would work just as well if the setting were Rome or some other place where Christians were under pressure."[12] Raymond Brown pointed out that Aramaic terms would not need to be translated into Greek in Galilee, nor would Jewish purification practices need to be explained to an audience there.[13] None of the various alternative settings for the composition of Mark has clearly won out over the rest, and some scholars still favor Rome as the Second Gospel's setting.[14]

CHARACTERISTICS OF THE GOSPEL OF MARK

The Second Gospel, the shortest of the four New Testament Gospels, is written in rough Koine Greek, probably the worst Greek in the New Testament.[15] The story line is episodic and non-linear—that is, no cause-and-effect, no climax. As Joanna Dewey has pointed out, there are multiple interconnections and overlapping sequences in both directions in

---

11. See, for example, Botha, "Historical Setting of Mark's Gospel," 29; Brown, *Introduction*, 127, 162.

12. Marcus, *Mark*, 33–37 (quote on 36).

13. Brown, *Introduction*, 162.

14. See, for example, Hengel, *Mark*.

15. See, for example, Nineham, *Saint Mark*, 40–41; Achtemeier, *1 Peter*, 2.

the storyline of Mark.[16] The audience of the Second Gospel consisted of Greek speakers whose vocabulary had been influenced by Latin. They were unfamiliar with Aramaic terms and Jewish purification customs but did know a number of terms from Judaism.[17]

Scholarly analysis in the past thirty years also shows that Mark was written in an oral register.[18] Structurally, "it consists of repetitive patterns, series of three parallel episodes, concentric structures, and chiastic structures."[19] Chiasms are turnaround or loop-like structures, where the text at the beginning of a sequence is mimicked by the text at the end. Mark is filled with chiasms. As Joanna Dewey has written, the text of Mark grew out of early Christian oral tradition about Jesus, a tradition that coalesced and developed quite rapidly, starting with separate stories strung together into a longer narrative.[20] In fact, Dewey has suggested that "it is the lack of a more literate chronological and topical order that Papias had in mind when he said Mark's story was 'not in order,' *ou mentoi taxei* (Eusebius, *Hist. Eccl.* 3:39:15). It followed oral ordering procedures, not proper rhetorical form."[21]

Drawing from the field of translation studies and from his study of the Aramaic language, Maurice Casey has proposed that certain passages in the Second Gospel are direct translations from the Aramaic and that several passages give evidence of mistakes that could only have come from the misreading of written Aramaic notes.[22] Casey concluded that the writer of this Gospel was bilingual in Greek and Aramaic, that he suffered from translation interference, and that he was a Jewish Christian from Israel who was writing to an audience that understood many Jewish customs and laws. He was not one of the twelve disciples, but must have had a disciple as his ultimate source.[23]

This juxtaposition of oral structure and written notes fits well with Papias's description of the writing down of oral anecdotes and preaching, and the mention of a memorandum or notes (*hypomnēma*) in the tradi-

16. Dewey, "Mark as Interwoven Tapestry," 228.
17. Brown, *Introduction*, 163.
18. See, for example, Dewey, "Oral Methods," 32–44; Botha, "Mark's Story," 304–31.
19. Dewey, "Survival of Mark's Gospel," 499.
20. Ibid., 500–503.
21. Dewey, "Survival of Mark's Gospel," 499.
22. Casey, *Aramaic Sources*, 85–86, 140, 191.
23. Ibid., 85, 136–37, 251, 259.

tion recorded by Clement of Alexandria. Apparently the preaching was first written down in the form of Aramaic notes and then translated into Greek, still retaining its oral compositional techniques and structure.

The use of notes, in fact, fits the way that writers composed literary works in the ancient world. In that period, an author would start a serious literary work by compiling preliminary notes,[24] much as I suggested for the composition of 1 Peter. Writers could carry these notes around with them on waxed tablets or on papyrus sheets. Often these notes were interlined or written in the margins of the author's working draft. The second-century writer Galen noted that authors often put alternate forms of a passage side by side on their working copies.[25] What sometimes happened, he noted, was that a copyist working with this rough draft would incorporate these marginal notes and alternate drafts into the copied text and create passages marked by redundancy and duplications.

The Second Gospel contains narrative repetitions in which the sequence of events in Mark 6:30-53; 7:1-23 is duplicated to a large extent in the events of 8:1-21: two feedings of the thousands, two lake crossings, two disputes with the Pharisees, and two discourses of food (defilement or bread and leaven). Both of these segments have Markan chiasms,[26] and both seem to have been constructed within an oral tradition. In the narrative sequence, the second set of episodes is supposed to have taken place outside of Galilee, but a close reading of Mark 8:1-21 shows a Galilean locale and the presence of Pharisees. In the same way Mark 10:10-16 is almost a duplication of 9:33-37, set in a house, presumably in Capernaum, although Jesus is supposedly on the way to Judea. I suspect that these duplicated passages are taken from two different sets of notes, perhaps of two different preaching episodes or cycles. The method of writing and copying in ancient literary works described by Galen—in which alternate versions of a passage, taken from two sets of notes, were put down in the working draft and later copied by a copyist who integrated them—would explain these passages of Mark.

Mark also contains a series of "sandwiches" or "bookends" in which unrelated material is inserted within a surrounding story: 3:20-35; 5:21-43; 6:7-32; 9:33-42; 11:12-25; 14:1-11; and 14:54-72. Johanna Dewey

---

24. See Strange, *Text of Acts*, 167-73; Bauckham, *Eyewitnesses*, 26.
25. Strange, *Text of Acts*, 178, 182.
26. Breck, *Shape of Biblical Language*, 149-51, 169-70.

has pointed out that these digressions fit comfortably within an oral mode of preaching.[27] In addition to conveying Peter's preaching, however, I think Mark sometimes used the sandwiches to present his own agenda or point of view. In the first two sandwiches, Mark's point of view is found in parts of the bracketing material: Jesus' rejection of his family and the healing of Jairus's twelve-year-old daughter. In the third sandwich Mark inserts the story of the death of John the Baptist within the story of the disciples' mission. Here he wishes to remind his audience of the contrast between John's disciples who buried John in a tomb, and those of Jesus, who fled.[28] In the fourth sandwich Mark has inserted his own material in the brackets, the story of the child in the house in Capernaum being taken into Jesus' arms with the key statement of Jesus in verse 37.

DATING MARK: THE CONVENTIONAL DATE AND EARLIER

Modern scholarly consensus places the writing of Mark between the late 60s and just after 70 CE.[29] One group uses the testimony by Papias and holds that the gospel was written in Rome shortly after the deaths of Peter and Paul (in accord with the tradition from Irenaeus) and before the destruction of the temple in Jerusalem in the Jewish war.[30] Another group places the writing of Mark in Galilee or Syria shortly after that war.[31] The latter group sees the Jewish war of 66–70 CE and the destruction of the temple as key dating points for the composition of the Second Gospel, particularly as reflected in Mark 13.

The problem with using the destruction of Jerusalem and the temple as a reference point to date Mark is that the Second Gospel, and the entire New Testament, for that matter, contains no specific reference whatsoever to the destruction of the temple.[32] In Mark 13:1–2 Jesus predicts that not one stone will be left upon another, but the burning of the temple in 70 CE is not mentioned in Mark, nor is any other aspect of the Jewish war.[33] There is a strong persecution theme in Mark, but it hard to use this as a historical dateline because Christians were persecuted from

27. Dewey, "Oral Methods," 35, 38–42.
28. Dart, *Decoding Mark*, 38.
29. Brown, *Introduction*, 163–64.
30. See, for example, Hengel, *Mark*, xi.
31. See, for example, Marcus, *Mark*, 33–36.
32. Brown, *Introduction*, 163 n. 93.
33. Marcus, *Mark*, 38.

the earliest years of the movement and at diverse places throughout the Roman Empire.

A few scholars place the composition of Mark significantly earlier than the Jewish war, based as much on the practice of Jewish law found in Mark as on its apocalyptic passages. Mark does not bear any evidence of the conflict that led to the Jerusalem conference of 48 or 49 CE that addressed the burning issue of whether Gentile Christians should obey Jewish food and purity laws and be circumcised.[34] In this earlier dating scheme, the apocalyptic passages in Mark are seen as a reflection of the Caligula crisis and its aftermath during the reign of Agrippa I.[35] Table 4 briefly compares the apocalyptical passages in Mark 13 to the events of 39–44 CE and 66–70 CE. Both periods provide reasonable fits in some places and more awkward ones in others. The "desolating sacrilege" is the most specific part of this passage and fits best with the Caligula crisis, but the persecution theme fits better with Nero's persecution of the Roman Christian community in 64 CE, unless Agrippa I's persecution of the Jerusalem Christians was more widespread than reported in the book of Acts.

TABLE 4. Principal End-Time Texts in Mark 13 Compared to the Caligula Crisis and Its Aftermath (39–44 CE) and the Jewish War (66–70 CE)

Mark 13: (verses in italics)	Events in 39–44 CE	Events in 66–70 CE
"Not one stone will be left here upon another; all will be thrown down." (2)	the temple remains intact and functioning after the death of Caligula in January 41 CE	the temple is destroyed by burning in 70 CE; Josephus says it was totally destroyed but stones remain intact on the Western Wall
"Many will come in my name, and say, 'I am he!' and they will lead many astray." (6) "False messiahs and false prophets will appear and produce signs and omens, to lead astray, if possible, the elect." (22)	activities of Simon Magnus in Samaria and Rome (Acts 8; Eusebius, *Eccl. Hist.* 2:13–14)	messianic pretenders are mentioned by Josephus (*War* 2:433–34, 444, 652; 6:313; 7:29–31)

34. Acts 15:1–34. For the practice of Jewish law in Mark see Crossley, *Date of Mark's Gospel*.

35. Crossley, *Date of Mark's Gospel*, 29–37.

The Composition of the Gospel of Mark

Mark 13: (verses in italics)	Events in 39–44 CE	Events in 66–70 CE
"wars and rumors of wars, . . . but the end is still to come. For nation will rise against nation, and kingdom against kingdom;" *(7–8)*	war between Herod Antipas and Aretas IV, ruler of Nabatea in 36–37; two or three Roman legions brought to Galilee to enforce Caligula's edict	defeat of Rome by the Parthians in 62 CE; civil war after Nero's death in 69 CE; Jewish war of 66–70 CE
"there will be earthquakes in various places," *(8)*	earthquake in Antioch and part of Syria in 37 CE	Tacitus reports earthquakes in 60 and 63 CE
"there will be famines;" *(8)*	possible one in Palestine, late 30s CE	
"they will hand you over to councils; and you will be beaten in synagogues; and you will stand before governors and kings because of me, . . . Brother will betray brother to death, and a father his child, and children will rise against parents and have them put to death;" *(9–13)*	persecution of early preachers in Jerusalem recorded in Acts; Agrippa I's persecution of the Jerusalem church; imperial edict of 41 CE limiting Jewish assemblies in Rome; persecution of Jews in Alexandria	Tacitus reports Nero's persecution of the Christians in Rome after the fire of July, 64 CE, including Christians turning in other Christians; no direct evidence for Christians persecuted in the Jewish war
"But when you see the desolating sacrilege set up where it ought not to be (let the reader understand)," *(14)*	proposed erection of the statue of Caligula in the temple in 39–40 CE	occupation of the temple sanctuary by Jewish Zealots in 67–68 CE
"then those in Judea must flee to the mountains;" *(14)*	flight of Peter from Jerusalem (41–44 CE)	Jerusalem Christians flee to Pella in the Decapolis shortly before the outbreak of Jewish war; other Jews fled to Jerusalem, not from it, in the first part of the war

NOTE: Events in 39–44 are from Crossley, *Date of Mark's Gospel*, 30–39; events in 66–70 are from Marcus, *Mark*, 30–31, 34–37.

MESSIANIC MOVEMENTS AND THE WRITING OF MARK

Messianic movements founded by a charismatic and apocalyptic leader are one form of what anthropologists call revitalization movements.[36] Typically, such movements rise and fall within a few years, a decade on the outside.[37] Messianic movements commonly fail due either to government suppression or failed prophecy. Both of these occurred in the immediate aftermath of the Caligula crisis of 40–41 CE. Shortly after the accession of Claudius, Christians in Jerusalem became the objects of persecution by Agrippa I, and several of the movement's most important leaders were killed or forced to flee. This sort of governmental suppression can be deadly to a fledgling messianic movement, but in this case the death of Agrippa I in 43 or 44 CE cut short the persecution.[38] More persecution occurred in Jerusalem in the early 60s when James the Lord's brother was killed, followed by the persecution of the Christians in Rome about the year 64 CE, but there is no record of Christians being persecuted in Judea just before or during the Jewish war.[39]

The Caligula crisis was the first real apocalyptic crisis faced by the early Christian movement.[40] Christians were waiting for the destruction of the temple, predicted by Jesus, and for his second coming. However, rather than the "desolating sacrilege set up where it ought not to be" (Mark 13:14) that these Christians expected, the whole Caligula crisis dissolved when the emperor died, and the reappearance of Jesus did not happen.

Usually, in such movements, such failed prophecy signals the beginning of the end. The rank-and-file members drift off, perhaps joining other groups or leaders that better meet their needs.[41] The switch of allegiance by Roman Christians from Christ to Simon Magnus at this time, even though described in legendary terms in the apocryphal *Acts of Peter*, fits this pattern.

Such a multi-faceted crisis would demand a response by the early Christian movement if it wished to maintain itself. Peter's journey to

---

36. Wallace, "Revitalization Movements," 267.
37. Wise, *First Messiah*, 32–34.
38. Schwartz, *Agrippa I*, 109–11, 145.
39. Marcus, *Mark*, 34.
40. Taylor, "Palestinian Christianity and the Caligula Crisis. Part I," 120–23; idem, "Palestinian Christianity and the Caligula Crisis. Part II," 13–41.
41. Wise, *First Messiah*, 35.

Rome may have been a part of this response. Simon Magnus's exploits would have been seen by church leaders as particularly dangerous to the faith of early believers in that city, especially in view of the fact that Jesus had not yet returned as promised.

The fact that apocalyptic fervor usually lasts less than a decade in messianic movements argues for an early date for the writing of the Second Gospel, which is so clearly apocalyptic in its message. Only by changing and restructuring itself can such a movement endure, but then it is no longer a revitalization movement. The start of this sort of change can be seen in the other two Synoptic Gospels that draw upon Mark, Matthew and Luke, where the apocalyptic message is already blunted.

PRINCIPAL THEMES IN MARK

Scholars have noted four important themes in Mark:

1) the so-called "messianic secret" and the role of Jesus as a suffering messiah;

2) the apocalyptic description of the end times (eschatology);

3) the role of the disciples; and

4) the role of the family of Jesus. The first two themes in particular are set within a framework of persecution. What is more puzzling, however, is the often negative portrayal of the disciples and the family of Jesus.

In a 1973 article, John Dominick Crossan suggested that the negative portrayal of the disciples, particularly Peter, James, and John, and the negative portrayal of the family of Jesus were "a manifesto from the Markan church, in whole or in part, against the jurisdictional and doctrinal hegemony of the Jerusalem church," and that "the polemic against the disciples and the polemic against the relatives intersect as a polemic against the doctrinal and jurisdictional hegemony of the Jerusalem mother-church."[42] In the next chapter I will show how the Second Gospel bears the indelible imprint of Peter's son. I will then show in chapter 7 that Crossan's second statement has some truth to it, and how these two sets of negative portrayals fit in with this familial relationship and why Mark wrote his gospel the way he did.

---

42. Crossan, "Relatives of Jesus," 111, 112.

6

Peter's Son and the Second Gospel

CHOOSING THE FIRST FOUR DISCIPLES

IN THE TIME OF Jesus, Capernaum was a fishing village on the west side of the Sea of Galilee (Gennesaret) and the home of Jesus' first two disciples, the brothers Simon (later called Peter) and Andrew, who fished on the lake (figure 4). Two other brothers, James and John the sons of Zebedee, also left their fishing on the Sea of Galilee and became disciples of Jesus.[1] In Mark, these four brothers are faithful followers of Jesus, held in marked contrast to Jesus' own four brothers, who were not. The initial choice of these four disciples also looks ahead to their preeminence among the Twelve, although later only Peter, James, and John retain their prominence. Peter is the first of the four; not uncoincidentally, Peter is Mark's father and Andrew his uncle. Fellow Capernaumites James and John were part of the same fishing cooperative as Peter and Andrew and thus well known to Peter's family.[2]

A very different story is told in the Gospel of John. Andrew, originally a disciple of John the Baptist, decides to follow Jesus after the Baptist calls Jesus the Lamb of God. Andrew then finds his brother Simon Peter, and they decide to follow Jesus. In John, the next two disciples chosen are Philip and Nathaniel, not James and John.[3] As the eminent Johannine scholar Raymond Brown concluded, John's account is quite plausible and must be taken seriously.[4]

---

1. Mark 1:16–20.

2. Luke 5:7–10. For fishing cooperatives see Hanson and Oakman, *Palestine in the Time of Jesus*, 106–9.

3. John 1:35–49.

4. Brown, *John (I-XII)*, 77.

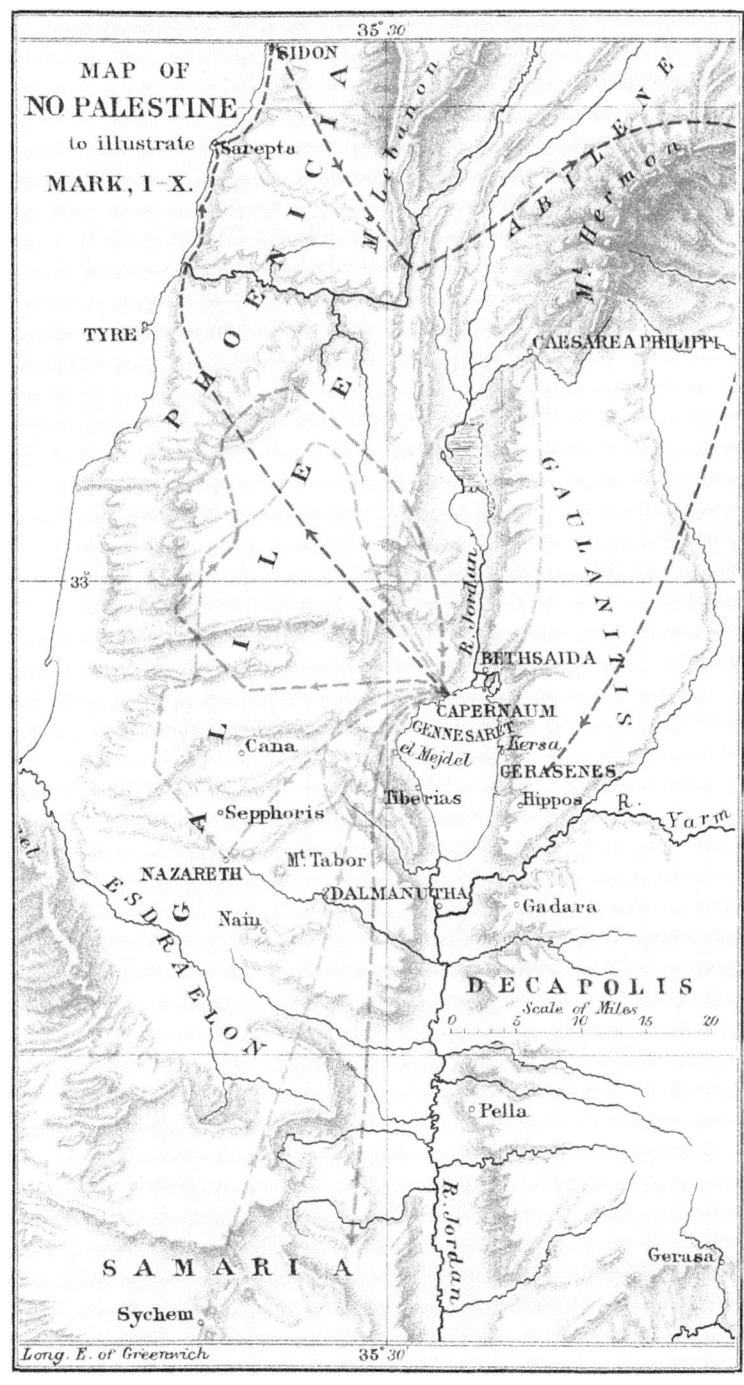

FIGURE 4. Map of Galilee and adjacent territories. Adapted from Swete, *St. Mark*.

PETER'S FAMILY AND THE HOUSE IN CAPERNAUM

Throughout the first half of the Second Gospel, Peter and Andrew's house in Capernaum is "the primary center of spatial orientation," the place of healing and teaching of the disciples in the narrative.[5] Peter and Andrew came originally from Bethsaida, a town on the northeastern edge of the Sea of Galilee.[6] Although the Capernaum house is called Simon and Andrew's house,[7] it is more likely that it was owned by Peter's mother-in-law, who would not have been living there otherwise.[8] A possible reason for this unusual situation is that Peter's wife's parents had no sons but only a daughter who stood to inherit her parent's property, a not unusual situation in Jewish families of the period.[9] If Peter's wife's father was or had been a fisherman, he would have married his daughter into another fishing family to carry on the business, and Simon Peter and his brother Andrew would then live there. The house would have been "theirs" in a functional but not a legal sense. At the death of Peter's father-in-law the property could have passed to his widow through the provisions of her *ketubbah* (marriage contract), or it could have passed to her as a gift made just before death.[10] Peter's father-in law could even have made a deed of gift to his wife in his own lifetime, as the father of Babatha did in the next century.[11]

The healing of Peter's mother-in-law in Mark is only the second healing recounted in that Gospel.[12] It falls outside the framework of the Second Gospel and is very personal.[13] After she is healed, the mother-in-law gets up and serves them. In doing this she is offering the hospitality of her home, and she is also the first human being in the Gospel of Mark to serve Jesus. The verb "to serve" used here is the same as that used a bit earlier in the Second Gospel when the angels "serve" Jesus.[14] This story

---

5. Breytenbach, "Mark and Galilee," 84.
6. John 1:44.
7. Mark 1:29.
8. Crossan and Reed, *Excavating Jesus*, 94.
9. Ilan, *Jewish Women*, 50–52.
10. Ibid., 169–70.
11. Yadin, *Bar-Kokhba*, 273.
12. Mark 1:30–31.
13. Hengel, *Mark*, 50.
14. Mark 1:13.

and the use of this verb highlights the preeminence of Peter's family and their relationship to Jesus in the Second Gospel.

Peter's mother-in-law was the grandmother of Mark. Since in the ancient Mediterranean world strong ties of affection existed between mothers and children,[15] Peter's mother-in-law would have been an important person in her daughter's and grandchildren's lives. She may in fact have been the caregiver for her grandchildren if Peter's wife accompanied her husband when the disciples followed Jesus about the Galilean countryside, as she did in Peter's later missionary journeys.[16] In Mark, unlike the parallel passage in Luke, "wife" is noticeably absent from the list of the family members the disciples have left to follow Jesus.[17] The idea of wives accompanying their husbands is very much in keeping with Jesus' teaching on the union of husbands and wives in Mark.[18]

The physical setting described for this house in the Second Gospel fits well with the layout of the first-century double-courtyard house with only one entrance that was excavated by archaeologists in Capernaum underneath a very early Christian church.[19] This fit is so good, in fact, that one scholar has even suggested that the writer of Mark visited this house when he was writing his Gospel in the 60s CE.[20] Mark 3:19 says: "Then he [Jesus] went home." Home, that is, to the house in Capernaum. This was, of course, the house in which Mark grew up, Mark's home. In neither of the other two Synoptic Gospels is the Capernaum house—Peter's mother-in-law's house—so central to the narrative, nor is it so accurately described. In the story of the healing of the paralytic, Luke incorrectly places tiles on the roof of the house but Mark correctly has the men *digging through the roof*.[21] The roofs of such houses were made of thatched reeds or straw covered with packed mud.[22] The incident of the men digging through his roof would have been a vivid memory from his boyhood, as were the

---

15. Malina, *New Testament World*, 142.

16. 1 Cor 9:5.

17. Mark 10:29–30; Luke 18:29.

18. Mark 10:7–9.

19. Mark 1:33; 2.2. For the excavated house at Capernaum see Breytenbach, "Mark and Galilee," 84, 85; Reed, *Archaeology*, 157; Moxnes, *Putting Jesus in His Place*, 40–41.

20. Breytenbach, "Mark and Galilee," 83–84.

21. The story is in Mark 2:2–12 and Luke 5:17–26. The roof is mentioned in Mark 2:4 and Luke 5:19, but this difference is not made clear in the NRSV.

22. Reed, *Archaeology*, 159.

crowds pressed around the courtyard and outside the door to see Jesus and have him heal them.

GEOGRAPHICAL PROBLEMS IN THE SECOND GOSPEL

Certain features have been cited to argue against a Palestinian Jewish source for the Second Gospel. First, there are supposed mistakes about Jewish laws and customs, but these do not require that the author of the Second Gospel be a Gentile, and as discussed by Joel Marcus and others, they may not be mistakes at all.[23] The most compelling arguments against a Palestinian source, and therefore of Mark's authorship, are the geographic problems in Mark.

The first occurs in Mark 5:1–13, where Jesus arrives in the country of the Gerasenes beside the Sea of Galilee. Here he heals a demon-possessed man who has been living among the tombs of the area. Jesus sends the demons into a herd of pigs who then rush down a steep bank into the sea. Gerasa, however, is thirty-seven miles from the Sea of Galilee. One possible alternative, Gadara, is five to six miles from it. Some later manuscripts substitute the name Gergesa, which may relate to a small town called Kersa or Kursa on the east side of the Sea of Galilee, but here there are no cliffs overhanging the water.[24]

Names fare poorly in human memory, unless they are important to the incident being remembered.[25] I would suggest that, in the repeated retellings of this story in the course of Peter's years of preaching, the name of the village became distorted into Gerasa, particularly since it was not important to the story line and because the name Gerasa relates to the Hebrew term for spirit-possession, which is the major theme of the story;[26] thus Gerasa is a likely substitution for the original name of the village, which I think was something like Kursa.

Another process that occurs as time goes on is sharpening, the exaggeration of certain details in a story.[27] The flight of the pigs down into

---

23. See Marcus, *Mark*, 19–21; Crossley, *Date of Mark's Gospel*, 159–205.

24. Nineham, *Saint Mark*, 153; Marcus, *Mark*, 342.

25. Bartlett, *Remembering*, 175; Allport and Postman, *Psychology of Rumor*, 84, 124–25; Campbell, "Systematic Error," 347–52; Higham, "Experimental Study," 51.

26. Derrett, "Spirit-Possession and the Gerasene Demoniac," 287.

27. Allport and Postman, *Rumor*, 84, 135; Johnson, "Retention," 218–23; Vansina, *Oral Tradition*, 9–10.

the sea became exaggerated with each retelling, so that by the time it was incorporated into the Second Gospel what may have originally been a gentle slope on which the pigs were feeding became a steep embankment over which they ran. The number of pigs in the story, 2,000, is also a clear exaggeration. A reasonable herd size would have been no more than about twenty or two dozen, and they would not have been far from the lakeshore: pigs require a lot of water and do not travel well.[28]

A similar confusion about place names may lie at the heart of the most glaring instance of mistaken geography in the Second Gospel. Mark 7:31 describes a journey from the region of Tyre through Sidon to the Sea of Galilee, and then through the region of the Decapolis. Sidon, however, is north of Tyre and Jesus is headed south. Wellhausen suggested that Sidon is a misrendering of Saidan, a variant of Bethsaida found in rabbinic sources.[29] This could have been either an oral mistake, as names are garbled in transmission, or a case of misreading written Aramaic notes, not unlike the cases discovered by Casey (see previous chapter). The use of "through Saidan" rather than the more appropriate "to Saidan" is probably another example of Semitic interference with the Greek—prepositions are notoriously difficult to master when learning a second language.[30]

Another instance of possibly mistaken geography in Mark is where the disciples go by boat from Capernaum on the west side of the Sea of Galilee to Bethsaida on the northeast side but land instead at Gennesaret on the northwest shore.[31] However, a contrary wind is mentioned in verse 48, which would have pushed the boat in the wrong direction.

In conclusion, the geographical problems in Mark are not compelling. They certainly provide no convincing evidence that the Second Gospel could not have been built on Peter's preaching or written by his son.

CHILDREN IN THE SECOND GOSPEL

What is particularly striking in the Second Gospel is the frequent and detailed mention of *children*, more so than in any of the other Gospels. Children had little status in the first-century Mediterranean world,[32] but

---

28. Hesse, and Wapnish, "Pig Remains," 240–42.
29. Nineham, *Saint Mark*, 203; Arav, "Bethsaida," 149.
30. Jobes, *1 Peter*, 7, 329, 334.
31. Mark 6:45, 53; see Brown, *Introduction*, 160 n. 83.
32. Malina and Rohrbaugh, *Social-Science Commentary*, 238.

the writer of Mark goes out of his way to give us details about them. In Mark, Jarius's twelve-year-old daughter is raised from death.[33] Matthew and Luke recount this story in much less detail, omitting the Aramaic words in Mark where Jesus calls her a "little girl."[34] In Mark Jarius refers to his child as his "little daughter," *thugatrion*, unlike in Matthew and Luke.[35] In the entire New Testament the use of the term *thugatrion* occurs only in two passages in Mark, here and when the "little daughter" of the SyroPhoenician woman is healed.[36] This latter child is simply called the daughter of the Canaanite woman in Matthew,[37] while Luke omits this story entirely. Elsewhere in Mark, Herodias's daughter dances for her stepfather and asks for the head of John the Baptist. This story is much briefer in Matthew and omitted entirely in Luke.[38] Also in Mark the child-aged son of a man is cured of an unclean spirit.[39]

The two most striking stories about children in the Second Gospel are in Mark 9:36–37, 42 and 10:13–16. In each story Jesus takes a child in his arms and either puts the child in the midst of the disciples or blesses the child or children saying (Mark 9:37): "Whoever welcomes one such child in my name welcomes me." In Mark, both instances take place in a house, in Mark 9 specifically in the house in Capernaum. The corresponding versions in Matthew and Luke do not specify the house in Capernaum.[40] Furthermore, both Matthew and Luke tone down "the unusual affection of Jesus for young ones,"[41] Matthew by making the blessing into a solitary occasion and Luke by substituting "infants" for children. The specific reference to the Capernaum house, Peter's family's house, and the vivid description of Jesus' actions in these two stories in Mark indicated to the early listeners of the Second Gospel that the child central to these stories—the child taken in Jesus' arms in the first story—was Peter's son Mark.

33. Mark 5:22–24, 35–43.
34. Matt 9:18–26; Luke 8:40–56. "Little girl" is in Mark 5:41.
35. Mark 5:23; Matt 9:18; Luke 8:42.
36. Mark 5:23; 7:25.
37. Mark 7:25–30; Matt 15:21–28.
38. Mark 6:22–28; Matt 14:6–11.
39. Mark 9:17–29; Matt 17:14–21; Luke 9:37–42.
40. Matt 18:2–6, 10; 19:13–15; Luke 9:47–48; 18:15–17.
41. Grassi, *Secret Identity*, 110.

Jesus' taking a child into his arms and giving it a special blessing is a symbolic act of adoption, similar to the adoption of Joseph's sons by Jacob in Genesis.[42] As Grassi notes, the child singled out in Mark 9:36–37 was likely known to Jesus, and the symbolic act of adoption served as a lesson to the Twelve that this child occupied a special place with him.[43] In this way this child was a successor to Jesus, as pointed out vividly in the passage: "Whoever welcomes one such child in my name welcomes me; and whoever welcomes me, welcomes not me but him who sent me."[44] *This is a clear-cut statement by Mark in his Gospel that Jesus had symbolically adopted him and intended him to have a key role in the leadership of his movement.*

It has been recently suggested that the writers of both Matthew and Luke intended their Gospels replace Mark.[45] To do this, they had to downplay or eliminate whatever authority was claimed by the writer of the Second Gospel (particularly if at that time "everybody knew" the writer was Peter's son). I believe the writers of Matthew and Luke intentionally altered the action and location in Mark 9:36–37 in which Jesus takes the child (Mark) into his arms, thus symbolically making this child, Peter's son, his successor,[46] and likewise the passage in Mark 3:31–34 in which Jesus says that his true family was inside the Capernaum house, that is, Peter's family's house. By downplaying or eliminating Peter's family and the importance of their house in Capernaum, the other two Synoptic writers attempted to circumvent the original source of these stories, Mark's Gospel, and the claim to authority by Mark, Peter's son.

PETER AND THE DISCIPLES IN MARK

The disciple Peter is mentioned twenty-five times in Mark, more frequently for the length of the text than in any other Gospel.[47] He is the first disciple mentioned, heads the list of disciples, and is the last disciple

---

42. Gen 48:8–15; see Derrett, "Children," 1–18; Grassi, *Secret Identity*, 108–9.
43. Grassi, *Secret Identity*, 110.
44. Mark 9:37.
45. Stanton, "Fourfold Gospel," 341–42; Dewey, "Survival of Mark's Gospel," 495.
46. Derrett, "Children," 17–18 for a discussion of the alterations in Matthew and Luke.
47. Feldmeier "Excursus," 59.

named.[48] Richard Bauckham argues that the prominence of Peter at both the beginning and the end form an *inclusio* around the whole story, indicating that it is Peter's witness.[49] He also found a plural-to-singular narrative device in Mark, which functions as presenting the perspective from inside the group of disciples.[50]

Rather than being an impersonal figure within the twelve disciples, Timothy Wiarda has discovered that Peter, unlike most of the other disciples, is distinctive and individual, displaying boldness of expression, impulsiveness, and is "more outspoken, more self-confident, and stronger in his sense of loyalty" to Jesus than the other disciples.[51] Even in his denial of Jesus on the night of Jesus' betrayal,[52] Peter emerges as a fully developed personality, unlike any of the other disciples. Such a characterization would be in keeping not only with the Second Gospel having been taken in large part from Peter's preaching but also having been written by Peter's son.

Wiarda has shown that there is no tendency to introduce individual spokesmen when portraying the disciples as a group.[53] In fact, outside of the Passion narrative, *only* Peter, his brother Andrew, and the sons of Zebedee amongst the Twelve are mentioned individually in the Second Gospel.

MARK'S DESCRIPTION OF THE FINAL WEEK

In Mark, the final week of Jesus' life occupies nearly one-third of the story. I proposed in the previous chapter that this segment of the Second Gospel contains some eyewitness material from the boy, now officially a young man, Mark. However, eyewitness accounts can vary and usually contain inaccuracies. Equally important, as time goes on eyewitness memories become inextricably mixed with rumor.[54] As historian M. W. Kauffman, studying the thousands of pages of eyewitness testimony from the assassination of Abraham Lincoln in Ford's Theater, wrote: "Virtually

---

48. Mark 1:16; 3:16; 16:7.
49. Bauckham, *Eyewitnesses*, 124–27.
50. Ibid., 156–64.
51. Wiarda, "Peter as Peter," 31.
52. Mark 14:66–72.
53. Wiarda, "Peter as Peter," 26–29.
54. Vansina, *Oral Tradition*, 6, 9, 55.

everything connected to the assassination is a matter of dispute. Doctors at the president's deathbed disagreed on which eye was swollen, as well as the ultimate location of the ball."[55] Kaufmann also noted that "as they [the eyewitnesses] talked to police and *to each other* [my italics], eyewitnesses found it difficult to make sense of their fragmented memories ... These differences would not have surprised investigators. In cases such as this, confusion and contradiction are the rule, not the exception. But fortunately for police, the identity of the assassin was not in dispute."[56]

It is significant that, despite all these differences, the overall outline of events and the identity of the assassin, who was well known to the theater audience, were evident from the eyewitness testimony. This conclusion confirms what many studies of memories of negative and emotionally charged events have shown, namely, that central details of the event or series of events are well remembered, while peripheral details are not.[57]

In Mark's case these were the memories of a young man, about thirteen years old, mixed with what others said and did, with rumors swirling around then and later, with distortions from retelling, and with his own particular agenda. Nonetheless, the overall outline of events was remembered by Jesus' followers: Jesus' triumphal entry into Jerusalem on a donkey, teaching at the temple, eating a last meal with his disciples, their trip to Gethsemane, Jesus praying there, his arrest by police led by Judas, his interrogation by the high priest and subsequent removal to the Roman prefect Pilate who then pronounced judgment upon him, Jesus' crucifixion, burial, and the empty tomb. These events are found in all the Gospels, and while Mark alone does not include any post-resurrection

---

55. Kauffman, *American Brutus*, 407 n. 11.

56. Ibid., 407 nn. 14, 15.

57. See Christianson, "Emotional Stress," 284–309; Conway et al., "Flashbulb Memories," 326–43; Berntsen, "Tunnel Memories," 1010–20; Schmidt, "Autobiographical Memories," 443–54. Very few of these studies have addressed the issue of significance, which plays a key part in how well an event is remembered (but see Conway et al. "Flashbulb Memories," and Schmolck, "Memory Distortions," 39–45). A person will remember a highly significant event better than a relatively insignificant event. Not yet appreciated or well-studied is the deterioration of memory for an event that once seemed highly significant but became insignificant as time passed (e.g., the O. J. Simpson verdict: see Schmolck, "Memory Distortions," 39–45). In our own time, only the death of President John Kennedy and the 9/11 events are equivalent to the death of Jesus to his followers.

appearances by Jesus it does contain the clear statement that Jesus has been raised (Mark 16:6).

Mark's account of Jesus' final week nonetheless presents several major disagreements with the other Gospel accounts, most notably with the Gospel of John. The first of these disagreements is when Jesus drives the moneychangers and sellers of pigeons out of the temple. Mark puts this event at the beginning of Jesus' last stay in Jerusalem, but the Gospel of John puts it just before the first Passover of Jesus' ministry, not his last.[58] John's account is more elaborate, including sheep and oxen as well as pigeons. It has Jesus make a whip of chords to drive the moneychangers out as he speaks about his Father's house. The account in John's Gospel appears to reflect what psychologists refer to as sharpening, or elaboration that affects stories passed down through greater spans of time, but its placement may be accurate. Mark puts this story within his own storyline, which includes only one Passover in Jerusalem. It probably made sense to Mark that this incident caused the priestly authorities to decide to have Jesus killed. In the Fourth Gospel, the priestly council, under the leadership of Caiaphas, decides to have Jesus killed after Jesus raises Lazarus from the dead.[59] Raising the dead would have been seen by many Jews of that time as a messianic act,[60] and thus a threat to the high-priestly authorities.

According to Mark 14:3–9, before Jesus went to Jerusalem he attended a dinner at the house of Simon the leper in Bethany where a woman anointed his head with a costly ointment. In response to some who were indignant at the wasteful use of this ointment Jesus defended the woman, saying she had anointed his body beforehand for burying. A more elaborate version is found in the Fourth Gospel.[61] Here Jesus is at the house of Martha, Mary, and Lazarus in Bethany. Mary anoints Jesus' feet and wipes his feet with her hair. The person criticizing the wasteful use of the

---

58. Mark 11:15–17; John 2:13–16.

59. John 11:45–53.

60. Among the Dead Sea Scrolls is 4Q521, sometimes termed a "Messianic Apocalypse," (see Vermes, *Complete Dead Sea Scrolls*, 391–92; Wise and Tabor, "Messiah at Qumran," 60–65). This is a messianic text that contains, unlike our modern version of Isa 61:1–2, a specific mention of the raising of the dead. This raising of the dead is also referred to by Jesus in Matt 11:5 and Luke 7:22 in response to who he (Jesus) is, making Jesus' reply a statement of his messianic identity.

61. John 12:1–8.

costly ointment is Judas Iscariot. It would have been highly unusual for a woman to anoint Jesus' feet and extraordinary for her to have used her own hair to wipe them.[62] Psychologists studying memory have found that as time passes people try more and more to make sense of their memories.[63] Therefore, as I suggested in the first chapter, when something is odd and out of place it may be from an original account, and so I think that John's version of this story is closer to the original incident and that Mark's version reflects repeated retellings by Peter during his mission, in the course of which the story has been changed to make more sense and the names of the women, Lazarus, and Judas were lost.[64]

In the Second Gospel what Christians call the Last Supper is called the Passover meal, and Mark says it occurred on the evening of the day the Passover lamb was sacrificed.[65] In the Gospel of John, however, the Last Supper occurs on the day before the Passover meal, and Jesus was crucified on the day the Passover lamb was sacrificed.[66] Jewish Talmudic tradition agrees with John, that Jeshu was hanged on the eve of Pesah (Passover), that is, the day of preparation for the Passover.[67] In Mark the priests hold a full session of the Sanhedrin in the small hours of the night after having eaten the entire banquet (including a whole lamb and four glasses of wine) only a few hours before.[68] To bring Jesus to Pilate on the morning of the Passover to be crucified goes against Jewish law and practice, for the priests would have been busy in the temple making their Passover sacrifices that day.[69]

In verse 14:12 Mark uses the sacrifice of the Passover lambs as his crucial date marker (he seems to be confused on the first day of the unleavened bread at that point). However, in the Jewish Mishnah there is a discussion as to whether a lamb slaughtered under its proper name is valid; this discussion *takes it for granted* that Passover lambs sacrificed on the thirteenth of Nisan are valid.[70] As Maurice Casey notes, "The assump-

62. Coakley, "Anointing at Bethany," 246–52.
63. Bartlett, *Remembering*, 93–94; Vansina, *Oral Tradition*, 5.
64. Coakley, "Anointing at Bethany," 255.
65. Mark 14:12.
66. John 13:1; 18:28, 39; 19:31, 42.
67. *b. Sanhedrin* 43a; see Herford, *Christianity*, 83–86.
68. Mark 14:53–65.
69. Josephus *Ant.* 3:249.
70. *m. Zebaḥim* 1:4, quoted in Casey, *Aramaic Sources*, 223–24.

tion makes excellent sense at the end of the Second Temple period, where there were so many pilgrims in Jerusalem that the victims [the lambs] could not possibly all have been sacrificed on the afternoon of fourteenth Nisan. It follows that everyone knew that many victims were sacrificed on thirteenth Nisan, and that this was accepted practice."[71] Thus Mark's critical date marker, the sacrifice of the lambs, could just as easily apply to the thirteenth Nisan, and then the date of the Last Supper in the Second Gospel would agree with its date in the Fourth.

Mark is convinced, however, that the Last Supper is a Passover meal.[72] I think this is because none of Jesus' followers celebrated a Passover meal that year, with Jesus dead and themselves in hiding. This last meal with Jesus was transformed in their minds, or certainly in Mark's mind, into the Passover feast. Possibly this became a group memory, but psychological studies have shown that groups are less likely than individuals to transmit false memories.[73] Therefore, it is more likely that this memory mistake, the common sort of error that psychologists call a retrieval error,[74] was Mark's alone, derived from his date marker of the sacrifice of the lambs.

As I will discuss in more detail in the next section of the book, the Last Supper was a Roman-style banquet, which was typically held in a large, richly furnished room with the guests reclining on couches (the couch is called a *triclinium* in Latin) facing each other. In the Second Gospel, Jesus says that the meal will take place in a large upper room, furnished and ready.[75] Traditionally, at such banquets, a guest could bring along his own guest to sit behind him on the couch while he reclined facing the other guests. This guest of the guest was called in Latin an *umbra* or shadow.[76] Also in the Roman tradition, fathers brought their near-adult sons with them to such banquets, with the sons usually seated at their feet or behind them but sometimes reclining.[77] I think Peter, a guest, brought his son with him at this meal.

71. Ibid., 224.

72. Mark 14:14, 16.

73. Stephenson et al., "Experimental Study," 175–91; Edwards and Middleton, "Joint Remembering," 423–59.

74. Brewer, "Memory," 21–90, found that 97 percent of the memory errors in his subjects were some type of retrieval error.

75. Mark 14:15.

76. Giacosa, *Taste of Ancient Rome*, 22.

77. Roller, *Dining Posture*, 159–61, 169–75.

The account in Mark makes no mention of any typical Passover food or rituals. Instead it has Jesus' statement that one who was eating would betray him and the disciples' response. Jesus then blesses the bread and says it is his body and gives thanks for the cup and says it is his blood of the covenant. Jesus goes on to say that he will not drink again of the fruit of the vine until he drinks it new in the kingdom of God.[78] Typically, according to Talmudic sources, the blessing of the bread and wine was given at the beginning of a meal.[79] In Mark, after this initial blessing the account skips to the end of the meal, a hymn is sung, and Jesus and those with him leave. What happened in between? Banquets such as these featured many courses, large amounts of rich food, and a good deal of wine. They lasted for hours.

This whole experience was probably overwhelming to a young teen who possibly had never seen such a large and richly furnished room in such an impressive private home before and had never eaten such rich and elaborately prepared foods. I think he ate too much and drank too much and then, woozy and overstuffed, upchucked on his tunic. Hurried away by servants, Mark was stripped, cleaned up, and given a length of cloth to cover him, with the intent for him to retrieve his tunic the next day after it had been washed. He probably missed a good part of the meal, some of it perhaps sleeping off the wine, but he was able to rejoin the group at the end for the singing of a final hymn and their departure to the Mount of Olives.

By now it was the disciples who were overstuffed and woozy, and the trek to Gethsemane was nearly two miles from the house where they had eaten (see chapter 8). When they arrived, they fell asleep. Mark, however, was awake, and it is his witness that forms the basis for Jesus' words and prayers at Gethsemane in the Second Gospel.

Recently Jerome Murphy-O'Connor has separated out structural doublets in these passages in the Gospel of Mark, giving two different versions of Jesus and the disciples at Gethsemane on the last evening of his life.[80] One source, which Murphy-O'Connor calls A, contains more ambiguities, mentions the disciples only as a group, and focuses on Jesus. This source recounts the mental distress of Jesus facing imminent death

---

78. Mark 14:22–25.

79. Noy, "Sixth Hour," 137–38.

80. Mark 14:32–42; see Murphy-O'Connor, "What Really Happened at Gesemane?," 39–58.

and is clearly very early. In the other source, B, Jesus is calmer and makes scriptural allusions. The disciples are specified as the trio of Peter, James, and John.

I think these two versions are an example of the dual drafts of certain sections of a literary work of the sort described by Galen mentioned in the previous chapter. The first, A, was probably taken from earliest notes of Peter's preaching, while the second was a later reworking. Because these stories were combined, the disciples fall asleep two times and Jesus prays twice (once from each story). The third time the text mentions the falling asleep of the disciples and the prayer of Jesus may actually have been the original outline of the incident, with Mark adding the two more detailed drafts when he worked further on his composition. All three were later integrated into the final text by a copyist, just as described by Galen. The copyist added such words as "again," "second," and "third" to make sense of the text before her or him.

When Jesus is arrested, Mark reports that one of those standing near strikes the slave of the high priest and cuts off his ear.[81] Mark does not identify the sword-wielding individual, and it is only in the Gospel of John we learn that it was Peter.[82] It is clear that the writer of the Second Gospel wishes to protect the perpetrator of this illegal act by not mentioning his name,[83] a natural impulse since it is Mark's own father.

Alone among the Gospels, the Second Gospel reports a young man who follows Jesus after his arrest, when all the disciples have fled. This young man is seized by those who had arrested Jesus but gets away, naked, leaving the linen cloth with which he has been covered.[84] As others have suggested, I believe that this young man was the writer of Mark.[85] Here was the clear identifier of the writer for the community of the Second Gospel—for "everyone knew" in Mark's audience that the young man was Mark, Peter's son. The Second Gospel's audience was already familiar with many of its stories through Peter's preaching, including Peter's subsequent denial of Jesus at the high priest's house.[86]

81. Mark 14:47.
82. John 18:10.
83. Swete, *St Mark*, 352.
84. Mark 14:50–52.
85. See, for example, Breck, *Shape of Biblical Language*, 171.
86. Mark 14:66–72.

Despite this hallmark denial by Peter, the Second Gospel contrasts the behavior of this young man and Peter himself, both of whom attempt to follow Jesus, with that of the other disciples, who have abjectly fled. But the young man is even more faithful than Peter, being the last to stay with Jesus and fleeing only when he is seized by the guards. The whole incident of the young man following Jesus is omitted by the writers of Matthew and Luke, who wished to avoid reminding their audiences of this claim to faithfulness by the young man who is Peter's son Mark.

In contrast to at least some eyewitness segments in earlier parts of Mark, the account of Jesus' trial in Mark and in the other Synoptic Gospels is a mixture of hearsay, rumor, exaggeration and a few scarce items that may have been factual. The idea that the Jewish Sanhedrin met in the middle of the night after the Passover feast to interrogate Jesus, as presented in Mark, is ludicrous.[87] However, the possibility of some sort of group gathering at the high priest's house the morning before the Passover is not impossible. In later Jewish Talmudic tradition, the high-priestly house of Hanan, that is, the house of Annas, was known for its "whisperings," thought to be its secret meetings or conclaves to devise oppressive measures.[88] In the oral telling and retelling of the story of Jesus' interrogation, this morning conclave of a few of Annas's allies could easily have become exaggerated into the whole of the Sanhedrin.

SUMMATION: PETER'S SON AND THE SECOND GOSPEL

All things considered, there are no compelling reasons why the Second Gospel couldn't have been written by Peter's son and number of reasons to support this conclusion. Peter's son would have spent his childhood in Capernaum and his youth in Jerusalem. In Jerusalem he could easily have acquired a good working knowledge of written Aramaic and both oral and written Koine Greek, enough to be Peter's interpreter and to go on missionary journeys. The strongly local and familial orientation in the Second Gospel, centered so much on Capernaum, and the surprisingly extensive mention of children, and of one child in an adoptive or successor role to Jesus in Peter's family's house, argue for this Gospel's close association with Peter and his son.

---

87. Vermes, *Passion*, 46–49.
88. *b. Pesaḥim* 57a; see Freedman, *Babylonian Talmud*, 57a, n. 2.

One asks, however, why Peter is portrayed so negatively in this Gospel if he was the source for much of it, as well as being the father of Mark. As Crossan noted, "Mark is severely and relentlessly critical of the Twelve in general, of Peter, James, and John in particular, and of Peter above all the others."[89] There is, in fact, a very good reason for this, which will be presented in the next chapter.

---

89. Crossan, *Birth of Christianity*, 557.

7

Mark, the Disciples, and the Relatives of Jesus

In the Anchor Bible's *Mark 1–8*, Joel Marcus states that:

> Mark's purpose in writing, then, is similar to that articulated by George Orwell: "My starting point is always a feeling of partisanship, a sense of injustice . . . I write it [the book] because there is some lie that I want to expose, some fact to which I want to draw attention, and my initial concern is to get a hearing (Why I Write, 5)." Mark, too, begins with a feeling of partisanship, a concern to get a hearing, a desire to expose lies and to draw attention to "facts."[1]

What was the cause of Mark's partisanship, his sense of injustice? To what facts did he wish to draw attention? In short, why was Mark *so aggrieved* that he wrote his Gospel the way he did?

Mark's problem goes back to the issue of succession in the early church and the decision of the disciples, headed by his father Peter, to transfer the authority and leadership from themselves to the relatives of Jesus, headed by James the Lord's brother. In Mark's way of thinking, his own family, the family of Peter, was Jesus' true family and the young Mark, symbolically adopted by Jesus as described in Mark 9:36–37, was Jesus' eventual successor. Mark was bitter and filled with a sense of injustice at this ceding of leadership by the disciples, especially his father, an action that prevented what Mark saw as the rightful chain of succession from taking place. Expressing these ideas openly would probably have gotten him kicked out of the church, at least in Jerusalem where James and the relatives of Jesus had their power base. Elsewhere, however, and expressed more obliquely in his writing, Mark sought to, as Orwell said, "get a hearing."

---

1. Marcus, *Mark*, 37.

MARK'S ANTAGONISM DIRECTED TOWARD THE RELATIVES OF JESUS

There is little doubt that certain passages in the Second Gospel reflect hostility to Jesus' family.[2] This hostility actually begins with the lack of a birth story in Mark and no mention of Jesus' genealogy or his Davidic connections. In Mark 1:16–20, four brothers: Simon Peter and his brother Andrew, James and his brother John, are picked as the first four disciples. They immediately follow Jesus, in contrast to Jesus' own four brothers, who do not follow him.

Following this, in Mark 3:21–35, Jesus' brothers and mother (notice the inclusion of the mother) come to take Jesus away from Peter's family's house in Capernaum because they think Jesus is out of his mind. Mark sandwiches this story with the story of the scribes who accuse Jesus of demonic possession, thus linking these two groups together in their common attitude against Jesus.[3] Jesus is inside with the family of Peter and other followers while his brothers and mother are outside, beyond the circle of true believers. Jesus identifies those inside, including Peter's family, as his true family: his mothers and brothers. These passages in the Second Gospel also reminded Mark's listeners of the "fact" that Jesus' brothers did not participate in his ministry and did him no honor, an important claim in a society in which honor and shame were crucial social values.

In Mark 6:1–6, Jesus is preaching in the synagogue at Nazareth and is met with astonishment. Mark has the people in the synagogue say "Is not this the carpenter, the son of Mary and brother of James and Joses and Judas and Simon, and are not his sisters here with us?" Again Mary is linked with the brothers and this time also with the sisters of Jesus. In the next sentence the people in the synagogue take offence at Jesus and, according to Mark, Jesus replies: "Prophets are not without honor, except in their hometown, and among their own kin, and in their own house." Other sources of this saying do not include a reference to kin or, originally, a reference to own house or household, making Mark's version

---

2. Mark 3:21–35; 6:1–6; 15:40, 47; 16:1. Those who have noted this include: Crossan, "Relatives of Jesus," 81–113; Brown et al., *Mary*, 54–59; Barton, *Discipleship and Family*, 68–83.

3. Kelber, *Oral and Written Gospel*, 102.

a clear indictment of the relatives of Jesus.[4] Again the relatives are set apart from those who honor Jesus, and the family house of Jesus is part of this denial of honor. By implication, this family house contrasts with the house of Peter's family where Jesus is honored. This is both a physical house, the one in Capernaum, and a familial house, the "house of Peter," which includes Peter's son Mark. It is not unlike the biblical house of David to which Jesus is supposed to belong. Pointedly, Mark's Gospel lacks mention of the Davidic connotations connected to Jesus' entry into Jerusalem, connotations that are found in the parallel accounts in the Gospels of Matthew and Luke.[5] The passage in Mark 6:1–6 is another part of Mark's claim, bolstered by the symbolic adoption story in Mark 9:36–37, that he and his family are the true family of Jesus—and thus the true leaders of the church—against the claims of the relatives of Jesus to that position.

Mark's claim is not based on discipleship as such, but on being Jesus' *true family*. This is a reflection of the importance of family and kinship in first-century Jewish society. Relationship to Jesus was probably the key factor in the choice of James the Lord's brother to head the Jerusalem church and an important factor behind the choice of Simeon the son of Clopas to be the second head of the Jerusalem church.[6] Recall that early in the next century, *family lineage alone* determined the appointment of one individual over another to the presidency of the rabbinical academy at Jamnia.[7]

A final accusation against the relatives of Jesus is found in Mark 16:8. This time it is the sisters of Jesus whom Mark singles out. In a parallel list to that of Jesus' brothers earlier in the Gospel,[8] Mark 15:40 lists the sisters of Jesus: Mary the mother of James the lesser and of Joses, and Salome. Mark does not bother to call them Jesus' sisters because in Mark's audience "everyone knows" who they are. The sisters are put with Mary Magdalene, who obviously was already firmly enshrined in Christian tradition as a witness to the crucifixion, burial, and resurrection of Jesus.[9]

---

4. Crossan, "Relatives of Jesus," 102–4.

5. Mark 11:10; cf. Matt 21:5, 9; Luke 19:38. Mark's version has the people say "*our* ancestor David." There is no specific reference to *Jesus'* ancestor David.

6. See Bauckham, *Jude*, 87 for the appointment of Simeon.

7. Johnson, *Genealogies*, 92, 94.

8. Mark 6:3.

9. For Mary Magdalene's place as a witness see Setzer, "Excellent Women," 262, 264.

Of the two sisters of Jesus Mary is obviously the most important, for she is also mentioned in Mark 15:47.

It should be recalled at this point that the apocryphal *Gospel of Thomas* and *Gospel of Mary*, as well as other apocryphal works, describe a conflict between Mary and Peter over authority and teaching (see chapter 3). In the Second Gospel, Mark acknowledges the women's discipleship,[10] but at the end of the Gospel the women are overcome by fear and fail to carry out the young man's command to tell Peter and the disciples. This command clearly sets Peter apart as the person with the greatest authority amongst the post-resurrection followers of Jesus and the women, particularly Jesus' sisters, as disobedient.

For Mark's purposes, it was quite appropriate that his Gospel end here with the women's, especially Jesus' sisters', disobedience, in effect pointing to *their rejection of this divine designation of leadership*. This is the reason why there is no lengthy post-resurrection ending in Mark.

SURROGATES FOR THE MOTHER AND SISTER OF JESUS IN THE GOSPEL OF MARK

Ross Kraemer has recently written on the numerous problems with the accounts of the death of John the Baptist found in the Gospels and in Josephus.[11] In the Gospel of Mark, Herod Antipas, who has John the Baptist beheaded despite thinking well of him, is totally manipulated by his wife Herodias and her daughter, although the daughter may be seen as an unwitting pawn of her mother. Interestingly enough, the daughter is not named in Mark, but from the Jewish historian Josephus we learn that Herodias had a daughter named Salome, the same name as one of Jesus' sisters.[12] Josephus however does not connect the death of John to Herodias or her daughter at all but says only that Antipas executed John because of the latter's influence with the common people and the possibility that John might use this influence to foment a rebellion.[13] According to Josephus, the destruction of Antipas's army by the forces of Aretas

---

10. Mark 15:41; see Setzer, "Excellent Women," 263. I wonder if these female witnesses to the resurrection once formed the end member of an *inclusio* in a tradition of women's witness to Jesus, with the beginning part of the *inclusio* being the original story of the midwife and Salome attesting to Mary's pregnancy (see chapter 1).

11. Kraemer, "Implicating Herodias and Her Daughter," 321–49.

12. Josephus, *Ant.* 18:136–37.

13. Josephus, *Ant.* 18:116–19.

IV, ruler of Arabia, was thought to be a punishment from God because Antipas had executed John.

Along with other scholars, Kraemer concludes that the story of Herodias and her daughter is not historically creditable. He argues that it was made up for Christian apologetic purposes to prove that Jesus was not John the Baptist raised from the dead.[14] Whether or not Kraemer's explanation is correct, it is evident that Mark had a compelling reason to present this unhistorical but possibly rumor-inspired story of a powerful and influential woman who was able, with the help of her daughter, to manipulate a hapless man so that one of the principal figures in the story of Jesus was killed. The hostility in Mark is tangible, much as it is in the later apocryphal works pitting Peter against Mary (see chapter 3).

In another incident in the Second Gospel Jesus calls the Syro-Phoenician woman and her daughter "little bitches" before he relents and heals the daughter.[15] This is one of the harshest remarks attributed to Jesus in all of the Gospels. Is it because the SyroPhoenician woman had dared to approach Jesus and beg, even insist, on healing from him for her daughter? No other Gentile in Mark is referred to so in such a hostile manner.

It has also been suggested that the Markan sandwich with the bracketing story of Jairus' twelve-year-old daughter in Capernaum and the inserted story of the woman with a hemorrhage for twelve years is an editorial statement by Mark, with the theological implication that, viewed from the perspective of the Jewish purity code, "women start to die at twelve and are walking dead thereafter."[16] Particularly significant, I think, is that the bracketing or intercalation of the woman and the girl puts them in a quasi-mother-daughter relationship.

Other women in Mark are presented in a very positive light: Mark's grandmother who serves Jesus, the poor widow in the temple, and the woman who anoints Jesus in Bethany in the final week of his life.[17] Mark's hostility then, is not to women in general but rather to mother-daughter combinations who demand and manipulate. One can't help but think this stems from his hostility to the mother and sisters of Jesus because of the

---

14. Kraemer, "Implicating Herodias and Her Daughter," 322, 342–44.
15. Mark 7:27; see Corley, "Feminist Myths of Christian Origins," 59, 65 n. 66.
16. Crossan, *Who Killed Jesus?*, 101.
17. Mark 1:30–31; 12:42–43; 14:3–9.

role these women played in the change of leadership in the Jerusalem church.

THE DISCIPLES: DUMB AND DUMBER?

A major argument long offered against a Petrine source for the Second Gospel is that the writer portrays the disciples negatively, including Peter. T. J. Weedon, for example, noted three successive stages of the disciples' relationship to Jesus: unperceiving, misconceiving, and rejecting.[18] Peter is fully a part of this scenario, which culminates in his denial of Jesus at the high priest's house.[19] However, one should keep in mind that instruction in ancient oral narrative "often was conveyed to an audience through 'warning examples of how not to behave,'"[20] a fact that suggests that Peter himself may have used this technique as part of his oral preaching. In any case, despite Peter's shortcomings we sympathize with him, in part because of the sympathetic presentation and explanations for his negative words or actions put forth by the writer of the Second Gospel, as would be expected if the writer was Peter's son.[21]

While some authors have noted positive aspects of the Markan portrayal of the disciples, in fact the Second Gospel portrays them, including and especially Peter, in a deeply ambivalent way, more so than in any other Gospel. This is graphically illustrated by Ernest Best who diagrams fifteen functions given to the disciples in Mark, of which two or three are essentially neutral, six are negative, and six or seven are positive.[22] This ambivalence, I believe, comes from, on the one hand, Mark's filial affection and, on the other hand, Mark's resentment of the decision by the disciples, most notably Peter, to cede authority in the church to James the Lord's brother and to other relatives of Jesus.

Mark clearly shares Orwell's "sense of injustice" and resents the decision of his father and the rest of the Twelve to cede leadership to the family of Jesus. By emphasizing and negatively elaborating on instructional elements in Peter's preaching to produce an at times negative portrayal

---

18. Weeden, *Mark: Traditions in Conflict*, 26–51, 163.

19. Mark 14:66–72.

20. Dewey, "Oral Methods," 42. The quote within the quote is from Havelock, *Preface to Plato*, 48.

21. Boomershine, "Peter's Denial," 56–58; see also Bauckham, *Eyewitnesses*, 176–77.

22. Best, "Role of the Disciples," 384–87.

of the disciples in the Second Gospel, Mark seeks to remind his audience that the Twelve did not have a clear insight into Jesus' teachings or his true nature. Only Peter is given the insight of who Jesus truly is, but then immediately backs away from it, just as he later denies knowing Jesus in the high priest's house.[23] By implication, Peter's backing down from leading the post-Resurrection church is as wrong as his earlier backing down and denial of Jesus.

DATING MARK IN REFERENCE TO THE RELATIVES OF JESUS AND THE DEATH OF PETER

The sharp edge of Mark's antagonism against the disciples and the relatives of Jesus argues that his Gospel was written not too long after the leadership change in the Jerusalem church had taken place. James the Lord's brother is central to Mark's antagonism and was surely alive when the Second Gospel was written. This puts the writing of the Second Gospel before 62 CE, the year of James's martyrdom (see chapter 3).

There is also no mention in Mark of Simeon, who was chosen as the second leader of the Jerusalem church after the death of James the Lord's brother, but only mention of Simeon's older brothers James the lesser and Joses. Simeon was probably the last child of Mary, Jesus' sister, and her husband Clopas and is said to have been martyred in the reign of the Emperor Trajan in 106 or 107 CE.[24] Reasonably speaking, this would put Simeon's birth about the year 30 or a little after. The lack of any mention of Simeon in the Second Gospel implies he was still a boy at the time of its writing (unlike his older brothers) and thus unknown or unimportant to Mark's audience.

Putting the writing of the Gospel of Mark before 62 CE places it outside the scope of the Neroan persecution of 64 CE. There is also no reference, either directly or obliquely, to the martyrdom of Peter in Mark, said by church tradition to have occurred during the Neroan persecution.[25] Nor is there any reference to the Jewish War of 66–70 CE. This leaves us with the Caligula crisis of 39–41 and the persecution by Agrippa I in 41–43/44 (see chapter 5) to fit with the apocalyptical and persecution

---

23. Mark 8:29–30, 32–33; 14:66–72.
24. Eusebius, *The History of the Church*, 142 nn. 1, 3.
25. Eusebius, *Eccl. Hist.* 2:25.

passages in Mark. This would also fit with the time that Simeon was a boy and thus unknown in larger Christian circles.

MARK: SURVIVAL AS THE GOSPEL WRITTEN BY PETER'S SON?

Joanna Dewey has noted how unlikely it was that Mark's Gospel survived at all.[26] She suggested that it survived because it is a good story, easily learned, easily performed, and easily transmitted orally.[27]

It is a good story, but I think it survived principally because there was a vestigial memory within the early church that the Gospel of Mark was an account connected intimately with the Apostle Peter and written by his son. Despite its manifest flaws and shortcomings, which the writers of Matthew and Luke saw and attempted to overcome in their Gospels, the authority carried by Mark lasted long enough for his Gospel to become enshrined in the Christian cannon, and thus survive.

---

26. Dewey, "Survival of Mark's Gospel," 495.
27. Ibid., 496.

8

A Crucial Question and Its Answer

New Testament scholar Paula Fredriksen formulated her 1999 book, *Jesus of Nazareth, King of the Jews*, around a crucial question: Why was Jesus executed by the Romans in a manner used for those who were guilty of political insurrection, but none of his followers were? Taking this matter further she questioned: Why were the followers of Jesus allowed to remain "ensconced comfortably in Jerusalem, directing a Mediterranean-wide mission without the slightest hint of constraint from Rome—or, for that matter, from Jerusalem's priestly hierarchy"?[1] Fredriksen, logically, answered the first part of her question based on the most obvious answer to the second part: Jesus' followers were essentially harmless and so were not constrained; thus Jesus himself was not doing anything politically seditious, such as calling himself a messiah, but the crowds gathered around him in Jerusalem for the Passover *were* calling him messiah, and so Jesus had to be killed to convince the people that he wasn't the messiah. As Fredriksen noted, most first-century Jews thought of a messiah as a Davidic military leader who would make Israel independent from Rome;[2] thus calling oneself a messiah could indeed get a Jewish leader killed. To support her argument, she noted that Herod Antipas, the ruler of Galilee, never moved against Jesus.[3]

This reasoning, that Jesus neither called himself nor thought of himself as a messiah but others did, logically answers her crucial question, but it requires ignoring all the messianic passages in the Gospels, including the witness of Peter and his son in Mark. It is notable that the first human to suggest that Jesus was "the Messiah," Peter, did so when Jesus and the disciples were in Caesarea Philippi, Gentile territory outside of the domain of Herod Antipas.[4] In this passage Jesus tells the disciples to keep

1. Fredriksen, *Jesus of Nazareth*, 9.
2. Ibid., 124.
3. Ibid., 215–18.
4. Mark 8:27–30.

silent on this matter, for it would indeed have sparked a forceful response from ruling authority.

Following Jesus' death, his disciples did proclaim his messiahship in Jerusalem, an activity that surprisingly received only rather ineffective notice by the Jewish authorities.[5] As Pierre-Antoine Bernheim notes:

> They [the disciples] claimed that Jesus was the one whom "God exalted at his right hand as Leader and Saviour, to give repentance to Israel and forgiveness of sins" (Acts 5:31). The priestly authorities must have considered the attribution of such an exalted position to an imposter crucified with their blessing as an insult and a challenge to their legitimacy. The provocation was all the greater since many among the eminent priestly families were Sadducees who did not believe in the resurrection of the dead. Moreover, these impudent people, instead of going to proclaim their message in the desert of Judaea or the mountains of high Galilee, were doing so under their noses, in the temple. Finally, a messianic proclamation of this type could easily give rise to disturbances of public order and bring down Roman repressions. *What is surprising is not that the disciples of Jesus were maltreated by the Jewish authorities, but that this did not happen to a greater degree* [my italics].[6]

Despite the inadequacy of Fredriksen's answer, the importance of her question remains. I believe there is an alternative answer, one involving the beloved disciple mentioned in the Gospel of John.

THE BELOVED DISCIPLE AND THE LAST SUPPER

The disciple "whom Jesus loved," or beloved disciple, first appears at the Last Supper.[7] The Fourth Gospel has this meal occurring the day before the Passover Seder, thus eliminating the scene presented in the Synoptic Gospels of the priestly authorities conferring with the Roman prefect on Passover itself when they were supposed to be conducting sacrifices in the temple (see chapter 6).

In banqueting practices in the first-century Jewish and Roman world, male diners reclined on couches, three to a couch, around a central table or tables in a Pi or inverted U shape. There is evidence that this shape was

---

5. Acts 2:31–41; 4:1–21, 26–31, 33; 5:17–40, 42.
6. Bernheim, *James*, 207.
7. John 13:23–25.

being modified into a T plus U design or an elongated U (see figure 5) during and after this period.[8]

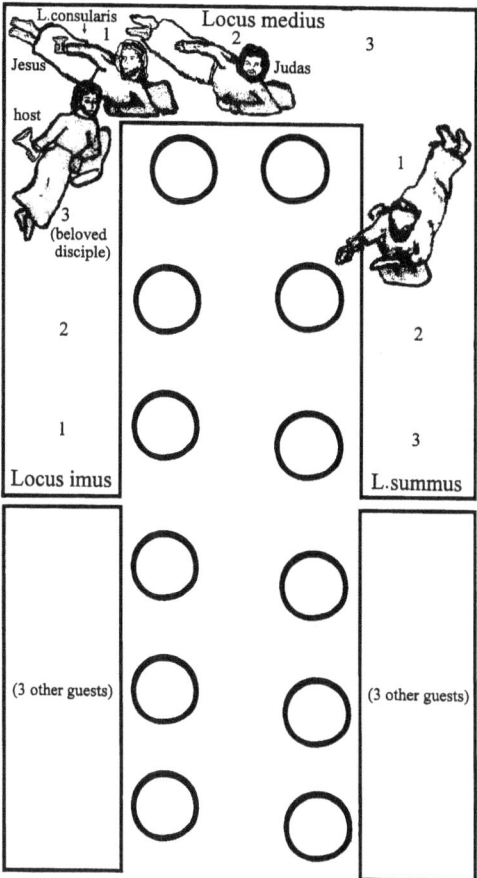

FIGURE 5. Sketch of dining positions at the Last Supper. Proposed seating plan is in an elongated "U" shape.

All guests were positioned strictly in the order of their status. In the typical Roman pattern, the guest of honor reclined on the end of the central or head couch where it joined the *locus imus*, the couch on the left; this position was sometimes called the *locus consularis*, because of the honor ascribed to it. The host lay immediately adjacent to him, on the innermost end (position 3) of the left side couch.[9] Later Talmudic tradition

---

8. Dunbabin, "Ut Greaco More Biberetur," 92–95.

9. Smith, *Symposium to Eucharist*, 17, 26, 136; Giacosa, *Taste of Ancient Rome*, 22–23.

had the host occupying the center position on the head couch with the guest of honor on his right.[10]

In the positioning order at the Last Supper, it is safe to say that Jesus would have been the guest of honor. The disciple whom Jesus loved was lying next to or on the breast of Jesus, that is, on Jesus' right, since diners reclined on an angle and rested on their left arm. This description indicates that the placement of diners at the Last Supper followed the typical Roman pattern, with Jesus on the far right of the head couch where it joined the left-hand couch (couches, whether of wood, stone, or masonry, were often continuous),[11] with the beloved disciple lying next to Jesus on the adjacent couch. The beloved disciple's position, number three on the *locus imus* or left side couch, was the place occupied by the meal's host, and in this case the host would have been the owner of the house, the householder mentioned in the Gospel of Mark.[12]

Jesus would thus have been flanked by the meal's host on one side and a second man on the other. This place on Jesus' other side was most likely occupied by Judas Iscariot, to whom Jesus gave a morsel dipped in sauce or wine.[13] To give the food to someone seated elsewhere, Jesus would have had to have gotten off the couch. However, there is no mention of that, although the text does say that Jesus got up to wash the disciples' feet and then reclined again afterward.[14] Nor does the text suggest that Judas was called over to a reclining Jesus, or that Jesus asked a servant to carry the morsel to Judas. As the group's treasurer or keeper of its money box,[15] Judas could well have been entitled to the place besides Jesus.

The text implies that the other diners were too far away to hear the remarks exchanged by Jesus and the beloved disciple, a situation that agrees with Katherine Dunbabin's observation that "the Roman design separates the guests and makes communication difficult between all except those on or adjacent to the central couch."[16]

---

10. Noy, "Sixth Hour," 138.

11. Dunbabin, "Ut Greaco More Biberetur," 91, fig. 7; Smith, *Symposium to Eucharist*, 17, fig. 4.

12. Mark 14:14–15.

13. John 13:26; see Brown, *John (XIII–XXI)*, 574.

14. John 13:4, 12.

15. John 12:4–6; 13:29.

16. John 13:25–26, 28; Dunbabin, "Ut Greaco More Biberetur," 95.

THE HOUSE OF THE LAST SUPPER

The house of the Last Supper was, according to earliest Christian tradition, on the slope of Mount Zion in the Upper City (see figure 6).[17] Archaeological excavations have revealed this area to be in the aristocratic quarter in Jerusalem in Jesus' time.[18] This location has met with skepticism by some scholars who have doubted that early Christians could have retained the memory of the place through two wars and the complete rebuilding of the city by the Emperor Hadrian.[19] But this locale is certainly appropriate for a house with an upper room large enough for the Last Supper, which was attended by at least fourteen adult diners (the twelve disciples, Jesus, and the host) and Peter's son Mark. It is less likely, though not impossible, that houses elsewhere in the city would have had a room of this size for dining.[20]

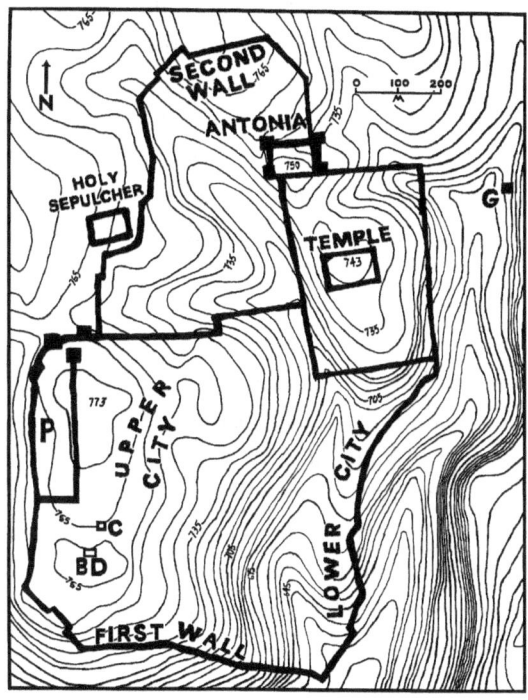

FIGURE 6. Map of Jerusalem at the time of Jesus' arrest. Note: contour lines are in six-meter intervals and scale is in meters.

C = Caiaphas's house; BD = beloved disciple's house; G = Gethsemane; P = Pilate's palace.

---

17. Murphy-O'Connor, "Cenacle," 303–21. An earlier version of this article is found in idem, "Cenacle and Community," 296–310.

18. Avigad, "Architecture of Jerusalem," 14–20; idem, *Discovering Jerusalem*, 83–191.

19. Bond, *Caiaphas*, 158–59, 198 n. 8.

20. In contrast to earlier notions, Jerusalem's Lower City contained some larger, multi-storied, and well-built houses in the first century CE; see Gibson, *Final Days of Jesus*, 51.

Early Christian tradition, graphically portrayed in the sixth-century Madaba map, also places the house of the high priest Caiaphas on Mount Zion.[21] Twentieth-century archaeological investigations have located the likely remains of Caiaphas' house, now in an Armenian monastery courtyard.[22] The traditional location of the house of the Last Supper, the house owned by the beloved disciple, is only about seventy-five meters (or about 245 feet) from the Caiaphas house.[23]

JUDAS ISCARIOT AND THE ARREST OF JESUS

In the Gospel of John, Judas Iscariot leaves the Last Supper while it is still in progress and goes out into the night.[24] Presumably Judas goes to the house of the high priest Caiaphas, for he has already arranged with the high priest to betray Jesus.[25] Yet, despite the physical closeness of the two houses, the high priest does not act immediately. He could have sent a relatively small force of his servants and temple police to the house of the beloved disciple where they could have sealed off the exits, entered the house, and taken into custody not only Jesus, but all of his top followers as well. It goes without saying that the best way to destroy a movement is to remove not only its leader, but as many of his chief deputies as possible. This is what the Romans did on other occasions when they acted against leaders of other popular Jewish movements.[26] This is what authorities hunting insurgent groups do today.

After Judas Iscariot's departure, the meal at the beloved disciple's house went on for some time, and afterward Jesus and his followers left the house (there were no police waiting outside), descended unhindered through the city, crossed the Kidron Valley, and arrived in the Garden of Gethsemane on the Mount of Olives, a journey of nearly two miles, well outside the city of Jerusalem itself. There is a good deal of evidence that this location on the Mount of Olives was in fact a cave, which contained an olive press.[27] At this time of year the press would have been idle and

---

21. Bond, *Caiaphas*, 156–57.
22. Avigad, "Architecture of Jerusalem," 14–20; Broshi, "House of Caiaphas," 57–60.
23. Murphy-O'Connor, "Cenacle," 319.
24. John 13:30.
25. Matt 26:14–16; Mark 14:10–11; Luke 22:3–6.
26. Fredriksen, *Jesus of Nazareth*, 149–51.
27. Taylor, "Where was Gethsemane?," 23–38.

the cave rented out to groups visiting Jerusalem for the Passover. Here, after more time passed, Jesus was apprehended by Judas and a contingent of the temple police, servants of the high priest, and Roman soldiers.[28] What is remarkable is that the police, servants, and soldiers, who carried lanterns and torches and commanded the entrance to the cave, did not arrest all of its inhabitants. Instead the disciples were allowed to flee into the night.[29] The police, servants, and soldiers could certainly have seen—and captured—not only Jesus but also many if not most of his disciples. However, rather than surround and arrest all of Jesus' followers, this armed contingent waited for Judas to identify Jesus, and *they arrested Jesus alone*. The high priest's men did not even bother to arrest Peter, who drew a sword and used it to cut off an ear of one of the high priest's servants, Malchus.[30] In fact, all of the actions of the high priest and his men seem to be aimed at *separating Jesus from his followers and apprehending him alone, away from the beloved disciple's house*.

THE BELOVED DISCIPLE AND PETER AT THE HIGH PRIEST'S HOUSE

After Jesus was brought to the high priest's house "another disciple," generally thought to be another term for the beloved disciple, was so well known to the high priest's servant that he effortlessly enters Caiaphas' residence. The Greek can even mean this other disciple "was related to" the high priest.[31] Peter also tries to enter the house, but he is forbidden entry until this other disciple vouches for him.[32] Peter stays in the courtyard with the servants and guards while the other disciple, obviously of a status above those servants and guards, disappears into the house. On the face of it, Peter's appearance here is remarkably foolhardy, unless he has confidence that his connection to the other disciple will protect him, despite the fact that this other disciple is known to be a follower of Jesus—the slave girl asks Peter if he is *also* a disciple. It seems odd that the door slave should know that this other disciple is a follower of Jesus, unless this other disciple is someone who is exceedingly familiar to the servants of

28. Matt 26:47–56; Mark 14:43–53; Luke 22:47–54; John 18:3–12.
29. Matt 26:56; Mark 14:50; John 18:3.
30. John 18:10.
31. John 18:16; see Hengel, *Johannine Question*, 125.
32. John 18:15–16.

Caiaphas and he to them—only in the Fourth Gospel is the name of the man whose ear got cut off mentioned, or the fact that it was this man's relative who questioned Peter.[33]

It has been suggested that this other disciple is Judas,[34] but Peter would have seen Judas appear on the Mount of Olives, at what might have been a private meeting spot known only to Jesus' closest followers, in any case leading the temple police and soldiers. After Judas kisses Jesus the latter is taken into custody and marched away. Would Peter really have trusted such a person to get him into the high priest's house where his own life would be in danger, particularly since Peter had just attacked and maimed the high priest's servant? The suggestion that Judas was the other disciple who provided free entry and presumed safety for Peter in the high priest's house makes no sense. Also, Judas is named in every other part of the Fourth Gospel, while the reticence in naming the "other disciple" exactly mirrors the reticence in naming the beloved disciple.

The beloved disciple, living so close to Caiaphas, was far more likely to have been known to the servants of Caiaphas and they to him. A much more probable scenario than Peter linking up with Judas is that Peter rushed to the beloved disciple's house and told him what had happened, and the two of them followed the soldiers to Caiaphas' house.[35]

The interrogation of Jesus by the high priest found in the Fourth Gospel is markedly different from the scene described in the Synoptic Gospels. In the Gospel of John, there is only Annas, the previous high priest and father-in-law of the present high priest Caiaphas, and several of the officers, who after the interrogation take Jesus to Caiaphas.[36] There is no mention of a transfer from one house to another, and it is likely that both the high priest and his father-in-law were in the same house that night. As mentioned earlier, in Talmudic tradition the high-priestly house of Hanan (Annas) was known for its "whisperings," thought to be secret meetings or conclaves to devise oppressive measures.[37] As suggested in chapter 6, this late night–early morning interrogation may have been such a secret meeting.

---

33. John 18:10, 26.
34. Charlesworth, *Beloved Disciple*, 336–59; Bond, *Caiaphas*, 135.
35. John 18:15 says Simon Peter followed Jesus and so did another disciple.
36. John 18:19–24.
37. b. Pesaḥim 57a; see Freedman, *Babylonian Talmud, Pesahim*, 57a, n. 2.

THE BELOVED DISCIPLE AT THE CRUCIFIXION AND ITS AFTERMATH

The next day, the fear of the crowds, purportedly the reason for not apprehending Jesus earlier,[38] did not stop Jesus' public trial, procession through the streets of Jerusalem to Golgotha, and very public execution. Perhaps the fact that so many people would have been at the temple, taking part in the slaughter of the Passover lambs (see chapter 6), meant not too many were on the streets to view the procession and execution. At Golgotha, the Synoptic Gospels describe how the women are looking on or stood at a distance,[39] but the Fourth Gospel has the beloved disciple standing near Jesus' mother, her sister, her daughter (who was also her sister-in-law), and Mary Magdalene by the cross.[40] Although these women would have posed no physical threat to the successful carrying out of the execution, for the Romans to have permitted an able-bodied man who was not a relative so close to the cross suggests that the beloved disciple was known and even had some influence with the soldiers or the Jewish authorities. From the cross Jesus puts his mother into the beloved disciple's custody "and from that hour the disciple took her into his own home."[41] Here for a second time, the house of the beloved disciple is presented as a safe haven, a fact that Jesus evidently realized, even as he was dying. It is also worth noting that Mary, as the daughter of a former high priest and a descendent of another high priest (Alcimus), would have been at significant risk for retribution from the rival high-priestly families, and that Jesus was aware of this.

On Easter morning, in the Fourth Gospel, Mary Magdalene goes to "the other disciple, the one whom Jesus loved," (note the combination of "the other disciple" and "the one whom Jesus loved") and Peter and tells them that Jesus' body was no longer in the tomb.[42] Peter and the beloved disciple run to the tomb, but the beloved disciple waits for Peter to go in first to examine the tomb's interior before he himself goes in. Why didn't the beloved disciple go in first? Ian Wilson has suggested it was because the beloved disciple belonged to Jerusalem's priestly hierarchy—priests

---

38. Matt 26:5 and Mark 14:2.
39. Matt 27:55; Mark 15:40; Luke 23:49.
40. John 19:25–26.
41. John 19:27.
42. John 20:2.

were not allowed to come into contact with dead bodies, which were ritually unclean.[43] When it was clear there was no body in the tomb, the beloved disciple went in too.

The house of the Last Supper is generally thought to be the house with the upper room where Jesus' followers gathered in the weeks following his execution and at Pentecost.[44] There certainly would not have been many houses in Jerusalem with a room large enough to accommodate all these individuals, *and* whose owner would have welcomed such a dangerous group as the followers of a man who had just been executed by the Romans for sedition. Here also, as time passed, the Jerusalem church had its center, and probably its church or synagogue in later centuries. A brief archaeological investigation just after the 1948 war showed what seemed to have been a second–third-century synagogue, despite the fact that the Romans would not have allowed a *Jewish* synagogue to exist in Aelia Capitolina (Jerusalem) at that time.[45] The niche that in synagogues holds the torah scrolls in this ancient synagogue pointed not east to the Jewish temple but north, to what is today the Church of the Holy Sepulchre, thought to encompass both the site of Jesus' crucifixion and his tomb.[46]

THE BELOVED DISCIPLE AND CAIAPHAS

During this period of Jewish history, the Roman prefect, Pontius Pilate, had absolute control over the office of high priest—Pilate even retained custody of the high-priestly vestments and only gave them to the high priest when necessary for ceremonies such as the Passover and Yom Kippur.[47] Nonetheless, Caiaphas and the Romans worked closely and harmoniously together—Caiaphas was high priest for nearly nineteen years, longer than any other individual under Roman rule.[48] However, Caiaphas was the son-in-law of the previous high priest, Annas. One of Annas's sons had already been high priest, and he had more sons who could become high priest if Caiaphas for any reason failed to satisfy the Romans. In fact,

---

43. Wilson, *Murder at Golgotha*, 151–52.
44. Acts 2:1–4; see also Mark 14:15.
45. Murphy-O'Connor, "Cenacle," 305, 307–8.
46. Ibid., 307 n. 10.
47. Josephus, *Ant.* 18:90–95.
48. VanderKam, *Joshua*, 426–36; Bond, *Caiaphas*, 43, 54–55.

two of Annas's sons did serve as high priest after Caiaphas was deposed, in late 36 or early 37 CE, and two more sons later in the century.[49]

Originally, according to the Gospel of John, the chief priests and Pharisees held a council a short while before the Passover. In this council Caiaphas said it was better to have one man die for the people than to have the whole nation destroyed.[50] Camillus Umoh has argued (rightfully I think) that what was really going on at this council was that the Jewish authorities were acting as local agents for Roman authority and that by putting Jesus to death they would maintain the political status quo, that is, they would stay in power.[51]

But why, as I pointed out earlier, did they stop with Jesus? Why not make sure this movement would be eradicated by at least arresting some of the chief followers as well? Caiaphas and his council would have realized that these chief followers could prove to be just as dangerous particularly if, as did indeed happen in the years to come, they (the twelve disciples) put themselves under the leadership of the equally Davidic brother of Jesus, James. What I think really happened at this council was that Caiaphas, by prophesying in his high-priestly role that one man, Jesus, should die for the nation,[52] was attempting to limit the actions of authority *to the removal of Jesus alone*, just as he would do on the night Jesus was arrested.

Keeping in mind that kinship relationships were crucial in the first-century Roman and Jewish worlds,[53] the best explanation for the remarkable behavior on the part of the high priest Caiaphas in the council and in relation to the subsequent arrest of Jesus—as well as the special roll played by the beloved disciple—is that the beloved disciple was a close relative of Caiaphas, as suggested in John 18:16. He was possibly a nephew or even a much younger brother. Caiaphas could not risk having the Roman prefect Pilate learn that his own close relative was one of Jesus' followers; if Pilate had discovered that such a close relative of Caiaphas was involved with the suspected insurgent Jesus, he would have removed Caiaphas from the office of high priest. This was why Caiaphas waited until Jesus and his

---

49. VanderKam, *Joshua*, 436–43, 448, 476–82; Bond, *Caiaphas*, 147–48.
50. John 11:47–53.
51. Umoh, *Plot*, especially xvii–xviii, 55–56, 88–95, 151–54, 196–97, 271–72.
52. John 11:50–51.
53. See, for example, Bernheim, *James*, 216–17; Bond, *Caiaphas*, 170–71, n. 26.

disciples had left the beloved disciple's house, and the city entirely, to send out a contingent to arrest Jesus, and why Judas was included in this force to identify Jesus so that the guards could arrest *Jesus alone*. It is also probably why Caiaphas rushed Jesus' appearance before Pilate, when so many of the priests were in the temple, preparing to slaughter the thousands of Passover lambs, before anyone could reach Pilate with accusations that Caiaphas had a relative in this movement or that the high priest had not acted quickly and decisively enough in dealing with this insurgent Jesus.

THE BELOVED DISCIPLE AND HIS PROTECTION OF THE EARLIEST CHRISTIANS

After Jesus' death, his followers were not harmed because this close relative of Caiaphas (that is, the beloved disciple) was so deeply imbedded in the Jesus movement that his house became the movement's headquarters. Caiaphas wasn't about to go into the beloved disciple's house to get Jesus' followers, although at first the disciples in their paranoia, did fear this might happen.[54] Caiaphas realized that moving against the followers of Jesus meant moving against the beloved disciple, and inevitably, the connection between the beloved disciple and Caiaphas would taint the latter to the point that he stood a very real chance of losing his high-priestly office. Only when Caiaphas was no longer high priest (during the reign of Agrippa I) was there serious persecution of the central members of the Jerusalem church,[55] and this by the king, not by the high priest.

This alternative solution to Fredriksen's crucial question better fits the information in the Gospels and Acts, allowing for a Jesus who did knowingly adopt a messianic role and his followers who likewise proclaimed his messiahship. In the eyes of imperial Rome, to be a messiah was to be seditious, for he would have been a potential military leader. Caiaphas's method of capturing Jesus, first by infiltrating the movement via Judas, then by taking *only Jesus* by night from a *neutral location*, and finally by getting him killed as rapidly as possible, served the dual purpose of

1) eliminating the leader of a potentially dangerous movement (a messianic insurrection would certainly have brought a military response

---

54. John 20:19.
55. Acts 12:1–3.

from Rome that would have unquestionably brought down Caiaphas and his allies, and possibly even harmed the temple itself) and

2) preventing widespread actions against Jesus' followers, actions that would have uncovered the beloved disciple's membership in the movement and jeopardized Caiaphas's position as high priest.

9

The Beloved Disciple and the Fourth Gospel

THE BELOVED DISCIPLE AS AUTHOR OF THE FOURTH GOSPEL

JOHN 21:20–24 EXPLICITLY EQUATES the beloved disciple with the writer of the Fourth Gospel, or at least the one who caused it to be written. The earliest manuscripts of the Fourth Gospel, dated by some scholars to 150 and 200 CE, are superscribed "according to John."[1] The earliest tradition that specifically attributes the Fourth Gospel to a disciple named John ("who had leaned on the Lord's breast") at Ephesus (in what is now Turkey—see figure 3) is found in Irenaeus in the second century.[2] According to Irenaeus, this disciple lived into the reign of the Emperor Trajan (98–117 CE).

Later tradition equated this John with the son of Zebedee, but as mentioned in an earlier chapter, traditions and liturgical texts, and a possible reference in the second volume of the early second-century writer Papias, exist that hold that John the son of Zebedee died a martyr's death along with his brother James or not long after, as suggested in the Gospel of Mark.[3] These martyr traditions fell into abeyance because of the much stronger tradition that John had lived to be an old man at Ephesus.[4]

Modern scholarship generally sees the Fourth Gospel as emerging from the Johannine community in Ephesus.[5] Recent studies have also shown that this Gospel exhibits a remarkable degree of archaeological and historical accuracy, quite separate from its christological or theological

---

1. Comfort and Barrett, *Complete Text*, 366–69, 491.

2. For a discussion of Irenaeus and his testimony see Schnackenburg, *Gospel according to St. John*, 77–81.

3. Mark 10:38–39; Hengel, *Johannine Question*, 21, 158 n. 121; Culpepper, *John*, 170–74; Boismard, *Martyre de Jean*.

4. Eusebius, *Eccl. Hist.* 3:18:1–3; 3:23.

5. See, for example, Brown, *Community of the Beloved Disciple*.

aspects.[6] The idea of the beloved disciple being John the son of Zebedee is now often discounted because internal characteristics in this Gospel argue strongly against such an attribution.[7] Four-fifths of the Fourth Gospel is set in Jerusalem and Judea rather than in Galilee, and many Galilean stories that John the son of Zebedee witnessed are omitted. The Fourth Gospel is associated throughout with the well-to-do rather than the poor, and it evinces a familiarity with the Jerusalem temple and Jewish rituals.[8]

Church historian Eusebius quoted Polycrates, a second-century bishop of Ephesus, as saying that John the beloved disciple was a priest and wore the sacerdotal (or high-priestly) plate on his forehead.[9] Polycrates had seven family members who served as bishops in the early church in Asia Minor, and this is from his family tradition. Although there is no record of anyone named John serving as high priest in the first century, psychologists studying memory and rumor have found that qualifiers commonly fall out as traditions are passed down. I think that Polycrates's family tradition probably originally contained the qualifier that John was a priest *in the family of* one who wore the sacerdotal plate. In time, this qualifier dropped out of Polycrates's family tradition. It is also important to note that even members of a high-priestly family can be called "high priest."[10] In a notable example, an inscription on a jug found at Masada and dated to 67–73 CE identified its owner as "great priest Aqavia," meaning "that the owner of the vessel was Aqavia, and he was *of the family of* High Priests."[11]

In Acts 4:6 there is a list that includes Annas and Caiaphas: "with Annas the high priest, Caiaphas, John, and Alexander, and all who were of the high-priestly family." Annas's sons were Eleazar, Jonathan, Theophilus, Matthias and Annas (or Ananus), but they are not mentioned on this list (although in two early manuscripts of Acts the name John has been altered to Jonathan to harmonize this list with one of Annas's known sons), while an otherwise completely unknown Alexander and a

6. von Wahlde, "Archaeology and John's Gospel," 523–86; Anderson, "Aspects of Historicity in the Gospel of John," 587–618.

7. Brown, *Introduction*, 369–71.

8. Parker, "John the Son of Zebedee and the Fourth Gospel," 35–43; Brown, *John (I-XII)*, xcviii.

9. Eusebius, *Eccl. Hist.* 3:31:3; 5:24:3.

10. Levine, *Jerusalem*, 354–55.

11. Yadin, *Masada*, 189.

John are. Annas's grandson John son of Theophilus was too young for this John.[12] The list begins with Annas and finishes with "all who were of the high-priestly family," and hence was not simply a list of random priests but an accounting of the high-priestly family, which at that time would have been composed of Annas and his close relatives and Caiaphas and *his close relatives*. Thus the John and Alexander who immediately follow Caiaphas on this list were most likely relatives of Caiaphas, not Annas. As several earlier scholars have noted, this John in the book of Acts is the most likely candidate for the beloved disciple.[13] In Acts 4:5–21 these high-priestly family members were part of a council investigating the preaching of Peter and John the son of Zebedee. Not surprisingly, given John the beloved disciple's presence, in this instance Peter and John the son of Zebedee were released with only verbal threats.

THE BELOVED DISCIPLE AND "THE ELDER"

A particularly puzzling question concerns the identity of the author of the Fourth Gospel and his relationship to "the Elder" named in Papias and in the second and third of the Johannine letters.[14] According to Eusebius in his early fourth-century *History*, Papias designates two Johns by the term Elder, the former obviously a disciple and the latter someone Papias himself heard.[15] Eusebius also mentions "the story that two men in Asia had the same name, and that there were two tombs in Ephesus, each of which is still called John's."[16] Eusebius concluded that one was the Apostle John and the other John the Elder.

In modern scholarship, Martin Hengel and Richard Bauckham, among others, see only one John in Ephesus, John the Elder. Hengel believes that the Fourth Gospel was written down from the oral teachings of John the Elder, who modeled himself on the beloved disciple.[17] Hengel suggests that the Gospel grew slowly when John was quite old, based on

---

12. See Barag and Flusser, "Ossuary of Yehoḥannah," 39–44 for this John and his daughter.

13. See Bauckham, *Eyewitnesses*, 449.

14. 2 John 1:1; 3 John 1:1.

15. Eusebius, *Eccl. Hist.* 3:39:1–10; see also Schnackenburg, *Gospel according to St. John*, 79–81.

16. Eusebius, *Eccl. Hist.* 3:39:1–10.

17. Hengel, *Johannine Question*, 94, 102.

the text having the smallest vocabulary of the four Gospels, and the Greek being elementary and repetitive.[18] Repetitiveness, however, is characteristic of oral presentation, and the elementary nature and limited vocabulary of the Greek may simply stem from the fact that the author is not a native speaker of that language. There are also many Semiticisms in the text, which agrees well with the fact that, although John was a common priestly name in Palestine, it was not a common name in diaspora.[19]

In contrast to Hengel, Bauckham thinks that John the Elder was the same as John the beloved disciple who was not John son of Zebedee but who was the author of the Fourth Gospel and who died, following Irenaeus, in the reign of Trajan.[20] Bauckham makes the point that Papias, when he mentions hearing the Elder and another man named Aristion (presumably a contemporary of the Elder), is referring to a time earlier than when he is actually writing, thought to be about 130 CE. Bauckham thinks this earlier time was probably in the decade of the 80s CE.[21]

However, there does seem to be a tradition of two very early Christian leaders at Ephesus named John. Eusebius obviously knew of it, and another document, termed the Apostolic Constitutions (or Constitutions of the Holy Apostles) includes a compendium of all the earliest bishops of the church. In its extant form the Constitutions is apparently fourth-century, but it contains various material from different times.[22] This compendium of bishops appears to be very early, because it lacks names found in the letters of Ignatius of Antioch, who was martyred in 107 CE.[23] In the letters of Ignatius, the bishop of Ephesus is named Onesimus, but in the compendium in the Apostolic Constitutions an earlier Onesimus, the one mentioned in the New Testament letter of Paul to Philemon, is said to be bishop of Borea (Beroea) in Macedonia, a place on the route of Paul's second and third missionary journeys.[24] The compendium has an Ariston, almost certainly the Aristion of Papias, as the first bishop of Smyrna. It also says that in Ephesus Timotheus (Timothy) was ordained

18. Ibid., 33, 47.
19. Ibid., 110.
20. Bauckham, *Eyewitnesses*, 416–19.
21. Ibid., 15–19.
22. Roberts and Donaldson, "Constitutions," 391–508.
23. See Staniforth, *Early Christian Writings*, 64, for Ignatius and his death.
24. Phln 10; Acts 17:10, 13; 20:4; Roberts and Donaldson, "Constitutions," 478.

by Paul and then John ordained by John (the Apostle). Because Ariston and "the Elder" are in an equivalent position in Papias, and Ariston is in an equivalent position with Paul's follower Onesimus in Borea and the second John at Ephesus (since Timothy is probably included because of Paul's letters) in the Apostolic Constitutions, I think this second John, not the apostle John, is likely to be "the Elder" in Papias.

A verse in the twenty-first chapter of the Gospel of John refers to what was obviously a widespread notion among the early followers of Jesus—that the beloved disciple would not die. The writer of this chapter attempts to correct this notion by saying, "yet Jesus did not say to him that he was not to die, but, 'If it is my will that he remain until I come, what is that to you?'"[25] The obvious inference is that the beloved disciple had indeed died and this writer sought to explain his death to the early Christian community, at least in Asia Minor.[26] Indeed, word of the death of the beloved disciple would have spread among the Christian communities in adjacent provinces, and many who were expecting the second coming of Christ during his lifetime would have been disappointed and fallen away.

In a famous letter that Pliny the Younger wrote to the Emperor Trajan from Pontus in northern Asia Minor in 112 CE, Pliny notes that some people accused of being Christians had ceased to be Christians twenty years before.[27] I wonder if this date, 92 CE, marks the death of the beloved disciple, and that Irenaeus's statement, that John the beloved disciple lived into the reign of Trajan, might actually mark the death of the beloved disciple's appointee John the Elder. If the beloved disciple was about twenty to twenty-five years old at the death of Jesus, he would have been born in about 5–10 CE and been about eighty-two to eighty-seven in 92 CE, around the same age or a bit younger as the second-century Christian bishop Polycarp of Smyrna, when he died.[28] Papias would have been correct in saying he asked people what the original "elders"—the disciples—had said and that he himself had heard the second "elder" probably sometime early in the second century. If this conclusion is correct, it was the second John, John the Elder, whom Papias is quoting on

---

25. John 21:23.
26. See, for example, Schnackenburg, *Gospel according to St. John*, 97.
27. Pliny the Younger, *Letters and Panegryicus*, 289.
28. For Polycarp's age see Staniforth, *Writings*, 158.

Mark. The quotation likely reflects the musings of an old man—thinking to himself of how Mark was Peter's son who hadn't directly heard Jesus preaching, how Mark's Gospel had been criticized, and then breaking into speech to the listening Papias on how Mark became Peter's interpreter and wrote accurately whatever he remembered. Those of us who have listened to the elderly tell their stories are quite familiar with this type of presentation.

TWO EDITIONS OF THE FOURTH GOSPEL?

Early manuscripts of the Fourth Gospel contain two variant readings in several places. One variant reads, "that you may continue to believe," and the other "that you may begin to believe."[29] These variants, combined with the dual ending of the Gospel in chapters 20 and 21, have persuaded a good many scholars that chapter 21 was a later addition and even that there were two editions of the Gospel.[30]

If this is indeed the case, the second John, John the Elder, would be a good candidate for the follower who edited the original text of the Gospel and added the last chapter. Most likely he was the person who wrote down the oral narrative of the beloved disciple in the first place, the narrative that constituted the rest of the Fourth Gospel. This procedure would have been in accord with Classical tradition, in which learned teachers (such as Socrates) did not write their words down themselves but their students did.

THE FOURTH GOSPEL IN RELATION TO THE GOSPEL OF MARK

If my interpretation of Papias's statement and the identity of John the Elder is correct, then this second John, as well as the beloved disciple, were familiar with the Second Gospel. Like the writers of the First and Third Gospels, the beloved disciple and John the Elder may have written this Gospel at least in part to correct what the beloved disciple saw were errors in the Second Gospel. For example, in Mark 9:37 in the Capernaum house Jesus says "Whoever welcomes one such child in my name welcomes me; and whoever welcomes me, welcomes not me but him who sent me." This

---

29. See Waetjen, *Gospel of the Beloved Disciple*, 5–6.
30. Ibid., 27–28.

is an important part of Mark's claim to authority, as noted earlier. But in the Gospel of John during the Last Supper at the beloved disciple's house Jesus says: "Whoever receives one whom I send receives me; and whoever receives me receives him who sent me."[31] Jesus probably said versions of this statement more than once, and John, in making this saying more general, probably comes closer to the saying's original intent.

As mentioned in chapter 6, John places the story of Jesus driving the moneychangers from the temple in the first year of Jesus' ministry, and the anointing of Jesus in Bethany at six days before the last Passover, in contrast to the two days before the Passover implied in Mark.[32] John also "corrects" Mark by placing the anointing in the house of Mary, Martha, and Lazarus and by naming Mary as the woman who anointed Jesus' feet (not head) and Judas Iscariot as the person who protested her actions. More importantly, the account of the final hours of Jesus' life in the Gospel of John is very different from that in the Gospel of Mark. As a close relative of Caiaphas, John the beloved disciple would have been an eyewitness to these events.

Another notable feature of the Fourth Gospel is that Peter, although playing an important role, is clearly subservient in belief and understanding to the beloved disciple. It is typical of storytelling based on recollective memory that the person recounting the memory puts himself or herself in a good light.[33] In this case the beloved disciple puts himself in a good light. The original ending of the Fourth Gospel at chapter 20 leaves Peter still in the shadow of disgrace after his denial of Jesus at the high priest's house. It is only the addition of chapter 21, the contribution I suggest came from the second John, John the Elder (who used a story circulating in early Christian oral tradition) that rehabilitated Peter.

It is clear from John the Elder's inclusion of Peter's rehabilitation in chapter 21 of the Fourth Gospel that he respected Peter and the important role Peter played in the early church. The apologetic note in the quote preserved by Papias, where the Elder defends the authenticity of Mark's rendition of Peter's preaching (if not its order), also echoes this respect. John the Elder, evidently, didn't bear any grudges against Peter or Mark, Peter's son. The same cannot be said of Mark for the beloved disciple,

---

31. John 13:20.

32. Mark 11:15-17; 14:3-9; cf. John 2:13-16; 12:1-8.

33. Neisser, "John Dean's Memory," 1-22; Vansina, *Oral Tradition*, 8; D'Argembeau and Van der Linden, "Remembering Pride and Shame," 538-47.

however, at least not during the time when Mark's anger at the leadership change was sharp and new, when he wrote his Gospel.

THE BELOVED DISCIPLE AND THE RICH YOUNG RULER

Does the beloved disciple appear in the other three Gospels? In Mark 10:17–31, as Jesus is starting his final journey to Jerusalem, a man comes up and kneels before Jesus and asks Jesus what he must do to inherit eternal life. After Jesus says he must obey various commandments and the man says he has observed these commandments from his youth Jesus replies to him, "'You lack one thing; go, sell what you own, and give the money to the poor, and you will have treasure in heaven; then come, follow me.' When he heard this he was shocked and went away grieving, for he had many possessions." Jesus then says "How hard it will be for those who have wealth to enter the kingdom of God!"[34] This is followed by one of the most vivid images in all the Synoptic Gospels, when Jesus says, "Children, how hard it is to enter the kingdom of God! It is easier for a camel to go through the eye of a needle than for someone who is rich to enter the kingdom of God." Seemingly Jesus relents for he then says: "For mortals it is impossible, but not for God; for God all things are possible." This story is followed immediately by Peter's statement to Jesus: "Look, we have left everything and followed you."[35] Here is Mark's vivid contrast between the rich man who will not give up his possessions to follow Jesus and Mark's father Peter, who notes that he and the disciples have "left everything" to follow Jesus.

In the Gospel of Matthew this story is repeated pretty much as it written in Mark, but in Matthew the man with possessions is termed "the young man."[36] Mark does not say he was young. In the Gospel of Luke, the story also occurs much as it is told in Mark, but in Luke it is a *ruler* who "was very rich" who asks Jesus what he must do to inherit eternal life.[37] These three versions are why scholars sometimes refer to this as the story of the "rich young ruler." The writers of both Matthew and Luke had sources besides Mark, and one presumes that they knew slightly different

---

34. Mark 10:21–23.
35. Mark 10:28.
36. Matt 19:16–30.
37. Luke 18:18–30.

versions of this story in which the man was "young" and "a ruler" as well as being rich and having great possessions.

There is, moreover, an identifier in Mark's story. In Mark 10:21 Mark says of this rich man: "Jesus looking at him loved him." The word for "loved" in Mark is the same used in the Gospel of John for "the disciple whom Jesus loved." This is Mark's way of telling his audience that this rich man is actually the *beloved disciple*.[38] Obviously Mark's audience already knew of the beloved disciple. John, the beloved disciple, was an influential member of the early Christian community and, as the foster son of Mary, probably supported her in her efforts to get her son James named as the leader of that community, against Peter and the other disciples. Although undoubtedly taken from a real incident in Jesus' ministry, this was Mark's attempt to contrast this "one whom Jesus loved" with his own father Peter, with Peter coming out morally and spiritually above John.

Neither Luke nor Matthew includes the phrase of Jesus loving this man in their version of the story. The other two Synoptic authors know who the man is, but they do not make any mention of this man's later role in the church for two reasons:

1) the beloved disciple did *not* sell his possessions, but instead used his house, his wealth, and his influence to protect and nurture the early Christians in Jerusalem; and

2) the key meaning of the story, that is, how hard it is for the rich to get into heaven, would have been blurred to the point that the story would lose its impact, particularly among the poor. Moreover, the other two Synoptic authors did not think it proper to hold up the beloved disciple to this criticism of Mark's, probably because they knew precisely why Mark put it the way he did in his Gospel; therefore they edited out Mark's underlying agenda, as they did in so many other places in their Gospels.

JOHN THE THIRD PILLAR OF THE EARLY CHURCH

Along with kinship ties, patron-client relationships formed the political and economic fabric of the first-century Mediterranean world. Patrons had "instrumental, economic, and political resources and can therefore

---

38. See also Swete, "Disciple Whom Jesus Loved?," 374.

give support and protection."[39] As S. S. Bartchy argued, the early Jerusalem Christians were a fictive kin-group with a few influential patrons who shared their wealth and opened their homes to their fellow Christians.[40] And as Jerome Murphy-O'Connor noted: "The highly idealistic common life (Acts 2.44–45) revealed by the most primitive source of the Acts of the Apostles . . . necessarily presupposes a spacious house and a generous host."[41]

John, member of the high-priestly family of Caiaphas and the beloved disciple, was the powerful patron and protector of, and economic support for, this early Jerusalem church. He was the third pillar mentioned by Paul in Gal 2.9. Because of this John's protection and support, the church in Jerusalem managed to survive and even flourish, despite its inherent challenge to the established priestly authority.

---

39. Moxnes, *Economy of the Kingdom*, 42.
40. Bartchy, "Community of Goods in Acts," 313–17.
41. Murphy-O'Connor, "Cenacle and Community," 305.

10

Concluding Remarks and Observations

For each of the three pillars of the early Christian church—James, the Lord's brother, Peter, and John—I have developed and presented an explanatory framework, one that I think clears up more of the uncertainties about these individuals than other hypotheses previously presented.

1) My hypothesis of the sources of the genealogies in Matthew and Luke, and how each genealogy relates to the families of Mary and Joseph, explains the inconsistencies between and within these genealogies better than any other previously offered hypothesis.

2) My hypothesis on the succession issues in the earliest church and on the writer of the Gospel of Mark being Peter's son explains more of the problems of the Second Gospel than any other hypothesis yet presented.

3) My hypothesized identity of the beloved disciple offers the best explanation as to why Jesus was arrested in such an unlikely manner and location, why he was executed so quickly, and most important, why the early church in Jerusalem was able to survive under the noses of what was undoubtedly a hostile priestly hierarchy. I have encountered no hypothesis or set of hypotheses in the scholarly literature that has done as complete a job in offering viable solutions to all of these problems.

Two key elements in my analysis are

1) seeing Jesus and his earliest followers as a messianic movement, similar in many key ways to other messianic movements in history; and

2) an appreciation of the importance that kinship and family ties played in this movement, as they have in so many other messianic movements. It is in this second aspect that biblical scholars have been particularly remiss, because in the modern societies of which they are a part, kinship plays a negligible role.

FORM CRITICISM, ORAL TRADITION, AND ORAL HISTORY

Both Joanna Dewey and Richard Bauckham have pointed out that certain underlying assumptions of form criticism are not confirmed by studies of oral tradition in real nonliterate or semiliterate societies. As Dewey says, "Form criticism has customarily assumed that the small episodic units to be discerned in the Synoptic Gospels were the individual units of oral tradition, and that Mark composed the Gospel from these bits and pieces of oral tradition and perhaps a short written source or two. All that we know or can infer about how tradition operates suggests that this assumption of form criticism is wrong . . . traditions are likely to coalesce into a continuous narrative or narrative framework quite quickly."[1]

Bauckham also noted that form criticism assumes that traditions about Jesus "passed through a long process of oral tradition in the early Christian communities and reached the writers of the Gospels only at a late stage in this process."[2] He goes on to argue that what Papias collected and what much of what the Gospels report was in fact oral history, not oral tradition, correctly pointing out the difference between the two—oral tradition has passed through at least one generation of tellers and hearers, while oral history has not.[3] As such, Bauckham contends, the Gospels contain much eyewitness testimony.

Although I do not think that Papias himself collected oral history, according to my analysis the Gospels of Mark and John do contain material from three eyewitnesses: Peter, his son Mark, and the beloved disciple John. Only one was an adult who was fully involved with Jesus' ministry from the beginning (Peter), and his contribution is found only in those parts of the Second Gospel that reflect his preaching. The other two eyewitnesses were a young teen and a relatively young man who were present only at certain points of Jesus' ministry and life. Their input is nonetheless valuable, even though the former was written with a distinct agenda and the latter was probably dictated decades later. Although subject to the distortions of memory over the long term, these accounts remain important sources of information, despite their limitations.

---

1. Dewey, "Survival of Mark's Gospel," 500.
2. Bauckham, *Eyewitnesses*, 6.
3. Ibid., 30–38.

NARRATIVE ACCOUNTS IN THE GOSPELS

As early as 1983 Elisabeth Schüssler Fiorenza called for an alternative way of reading the texts and traditions of Jesus and his movement, a way that focused on the narrative itself and the people involved.[4] Because there is eyewitness material in the Gospels of Mark and John, a close examination of the narrative itself is crucial for evaluating the accounts, especially that of the last evening of Jesus' life, one of the most important parts of all the Gospels. These narrative accounts are also crucial for discovering the identity of the beloved disciple and, through analysis, his significance in the early Christian movement. My analysis also shows that the narrative material contains key clues to the writer of the Second Gospel and a realistic way to evaluate the differences between the accounts in Mark and John concerning the last week of Jesus' life.

The narrative also provides a key indication that Mary the mother of John Mark in the book of Acts was in fact Peter's wife. This discovery, along with her recognition as the co-elect in 1 Peter, sheds new light on this important woman. It is clear that she was an influential person in the early church and a vital partner in Peter's mission and ministry.

THE IMPORTANCE OF JESUS' GENEALOGY

Although to modern sensibilities, the idea that a person's genealogy should determine their social, political, and even religious importance is extremely hard to fathom, it was not so to the people of Jesus' time. Had Jesus been a nobody, no more than a simple Galilean peasant, the Pharisees would have ignored him as simply another of the people of the land.[5] Had he been a nobody the priestly hierarchy would probably have had him whipped and thrown out of Jerusalem.

The fact that Jesus was, at least in popular perspective, a descendent of King David on his father's side and a descendent of a high-priestly line on his mother's put him in a potential position of authority, for the common people would have thought that his genealogy qualified him to be a messiah. Jesus clearly played on this special position when in the last week of his life he entered Jerusalem on a donkey to fulfill the prediction in Zech 9:9. Not only did this action remind the populace of this particu-

---

4. Schüssler Fiorenza, *In Memory of Her*, 152.
5. Dijkhuizen, "Investigation," 35.

lar prophecy of Zechariah's, it also reminded them of Zechariah's other prophecy—the one related to Jesus' genealogy (Zech 4:13).

From another point of view, however, his genealogical attributes placed Jesus in a special position of vulnerability. Jesus' paternal Davidic descent would have made him a particular danger to the "sons of Seth," represented by the former but still powerful high priest Annas (Ananus) and his sons. On his maternal side Jesus was heir to whatever animosities existed between his grandfather Joseph ben Elim and Joseph's kinsman the high priest Matthias ben Theophilus, and that of the house of Boethus particularly if, as mentioned in chapter 2, the high priest Joseph Caiaphas was an offshoot of the house of Boethus. This animosity might even extend back further in time, if Josephus is correct there being a connection between the fleeing or driving out of Onias IV from Jerusalem and the appointment of Alcimus as high priest.[6]

Undoubtedly Jesus was a charismatic leader, and any charismatic leader who had such potential to be a messiah would have been seen as a threat by the high-priestly authorities who, as Richard Horsley has pointed out, derived their power from Rome and who cooperated with the Romans in dominating the Jewish people in Palestine.[7] It was this narrow circle of priestly aristocrats, endeavoring to hold onto their authority, who wanted to kill this potential messiah so they could keep themselves in power under the aegis of their imperial Roman masters. Fearing Jesus' popularity with the people however, these high-priestly aristocrats made sure it was the Roman prefect who crucified Jesus as an insurgent—as the Romans always did with any real or potential insurgents—rather than bring condemnation from the ordinary Jewish people upon themselves.

---

6. Josephus, *Ant.* 12:387–88; 20:235–36.
7. Horsley, "High Priests," 23–55.

BIBLIOGRAPHY

Achtemeier, Paul J. *1 Peter: A Commentary on 1 Peter*. Minneapolis: Fortress, 1996.
Allport, Gordon W., and Leo J. Postman. "The Basic Psychology of Rumor." *Transactions of the New York Academy of Sciences*, 11th ser., 8 (1945) 61-81.
———. *The Psychology of Rumor*. New York: Holt, 1947.
Anderson, Paul N. "Aspects of Historicity in the Gospel of John: Implications for Investigations of Jesus and Archaeology." In *Jesus and Archaeology*, edited by James H. Charlesworth, 587-618. Grand Rapids: Eerdmans, 2006.
Applegate, Judith K. "The Co-elect Woman of 1 Peter." *NTS* 38 (1992) 587-604.
Arav, Rami. "Bethsaida." In *Jesus and Archaeology*, edited by James H. Charlesworth, 145-66. Grand Rapids: Eerdmans, 2006.
Avigad, N. "The Architecture of Jerusalem in the Second Temple Period." In *Jerusalem Revealed: Archaeology of the Holy City 1968-1974*, edited by Yigael Yadin, 14-20. Jerusalem: Israel Exploration Society, 1975.
———. *Discovering Jerusalem*. Nashville: Thomas Nelson, 1983.
Barag, Dan, and David Flusser. "The Ossuary of Yehoḥannah Granddaughter of the High Priest Theophilus." *IEJ* 36 (1986) 39-44.
Barber, Elizabeth W., and Paul T. Barber. *When They Severed Earth from Sky: How the Human Mind Shapes Myth*. Princeton: Princeton University Press, 2004.
Bartchy, S. Scot. "Community of Goods in Acts: Idealization or Social Reality? In *The Future of Early Christianity: Essays in Honor of Helmut Koester*, edited by B. A. Pearson, 309-18. Minneapolis: Fortress, 1991.
Bartlett, Frederic C. *Remembering: A Study in Experimental and Social Psychology*. Cambridge: Cambridge University Press, 1932.
Barton, Stephen C. *Discipleship and Family Ties in Mark and Matthew*. SNTSMS 80. Cambridge: Cambridge University Press, 1994.
Batey, Richard A. "Is Not This the Carpenter?" *NTS* 30 (1984) 249-58.
Bauckham, Richard. *Gospel Women: Studies of the Named Women in the Gospels*. Grand Rapids: Eerdmans, 2002.
———. "James and the Gentiles (Acts 15:13-21)." In *History, Literature and Society in the Book of Acts*, edited by Ben Witherington III, 154-84. Cambridge: Cambridge University Press, 1996.
———. "James and the Jerusalem Church." In *The Book of Acts in Its Palestinian Setting*, edited by Richard Bauckham, 415-80. Vol. 4 of *The Book of Acts in Its First Century Setting*. Edited by Bruce W. Winter. Grand Rapids: Eerdmans, 1995.
———. *Jesus and the Eyewitnesses*. Grand Rapids: Eerdmans, 2006.

———. *Jude and the Relatives of Jesus in the Early Church.* Edinburgh: T & T Clark, 1990.
———. "Mary of Clopas (John 19:25)." In *Women in the Biblical Tradition*, edited by G. J. Brooke, 231–55. Lewiston, NY: Mellen, 1992.
———. "Salome the Sister of Jesus, Salome the Disciple of Jesus, and the Secret Gospel of Mark." *NovT* 33 (1991) 245–75.
Bernheim, Pierre-Antoine. *James, Brother of Jesus.* London: SCM, 1997.
Berntsen, Dorthe. "Tunnel Memories for Autobiographical Events: Central Details Are Remembered More Frequently from Shocking Than from Happy Experiences." *Memory and Cognition* 30 (2002) 1010–20.
Best, Ernest. *1 Peter.* NCB. Grand Rapids: Eerdmans, 1971.
———. "The Role of the Disciples in Mark." *NTS* 23 (1976/77) 377–401.
Black, C. Clifton. *Mark: Images of an Apostolic Interpreter.* Edinburgh: T & T Clark, 2001.
Blair, H. A. "Matthew 1,16 and the Matthaean Genealogy." *TU* 87 (1964) 149–54.
Blinzler, J. *Die Brüder und Schwestern Jesu.* 2d ed. SBS 21. Stuttgart: Katholisches Bibelwerk, 1967.
Boismard, M.-É. *Le Martyre de Jean L'Apôtre.* CahRB 35. Paris: J. Gabalda, 1996.
Bond, Helen K. *Caiaphas: Friend of Rome and Judge of Jesus?* Louisville, KY: Westminster John Knox, 2004.
Boomershine, Thomas E. "Peter's Denial as Polemic or Confession: The Implications of Media Criticism for Biblical Hermeneutics." *Semeia* 39 (1987) 47–68.
Botha, Pieter J. J. "The Historical Setting of Mark's Gospel: Problems and Possibilities." *JSNT* 51 (1993) 27–55.
———. "Mark's Story as Oral Traditional Literature: Rethinking the Transmission of Some Traditions about Jesus." *HvTSt* 47 (1991) 304–31.
Breck, John. *The Shape of Biblical Language: Chiasmus in the Scriptures and Beyond.* Crestwood, NY: St. Vladimir's Seminary Press, 1994.
Brewer, William F. "Memory for Randomly Sampled Autobiographical Events." In *Remembering Reconsidered: Ecological and Traditional Approaches to the Study of Memory*, edited by Ulric Neisser and Eugene Winograd, 21–90. Cambridge: Cambridge University Press, 1988.
Breytenbach, Cilliers. "Mark and Galilee: Text World and Historical World." In *Galilee through the Centuries: Confluence of Cultures*, edited by Eric M. Meyers, 75–85. Winona Lake, IN: Eisenbrauns, 1999.
Brody, Robert. "Caiaphas and Cantheras." Appendix IV in Daniel R. Schwartz, *Agrippa I: The Last King of Judaea*, 190–95. TSAJ 23. Tübingen: Mohr Siebeck, 1990.
Broshi, M. "Excavations in the House of Caiaphas, Mount Zion." In *Jerusalem Revealed: Archaeology of the Holy City 1968–1974*, edited by Yigael Yadin, 57–60. Jerusalem: Israel Exploration Society, 1975.
Brown, Raymond E. *The Birth of the Messiah.* Garden City, NY: Doubleday, 1977.
———. *The Community of the Beloved Disciple: The Life, Loves, and Hates of an Individual Church in New Testament Times.* New York: Paulist, 1979.
———. *The Gospel according to John (I–XII).* AB 29. New York: Doubleday, 1966.
———. *The Gospel According to John (XIII–XXI).* AB 29a. New York: Doubleday, 1970.
———. *An Introduction to the New Testament.* ABRL. New York: Doubleday, 1997.
Brown, Raymond E. et al., editors. *Mary in the New Testament.* New York: Paulist, 1978.
Buchanan, George W. "Jesus and the Upper Class." *NovT* 7 (1964) 195–209.
Campbell, Donald T. "Systematic Error on the Part of Human Links in Communications Systems." *Information and Control* 1 (1958) 334–69.

Campbell, K. M., "What Was Jesus' Occupation?" *JETS* 48 (2005) 501–19.
Casey, Maurice. *Aramaic Sources of Mark's Gospel*. Cambridge: Cambridge University Press, 1998.
Chancey, Mark, and Eric M. Meyers. "How Jewish Was Sepphoris in Jesus' Time?" *BAR* 26, 4 (2000) 18–33, 61.
Charles, R. H. "Fragments of a Zadokite Work: Introduction." *APOT* 2:785–95.
Charlesworth, James H. *The Beloved Disciple Whose Witness Validates the Gospel of John?* Valley Forge, PA: Trinity, 1995.
Chilton, Bruce, and Craig A. Evans, editors. *James the Just and Christian Origins*. NovTSup 98. Leiden: Brill, 1999.
Chilton, Bruce, and Jacob Neusner, editors. *The Brother of Jesus: James the Just and His Mission*. Louisville, KY: Westminster John Knox, 2001.
Christianson, Sven-Åke. "Emotional Stress and Eyewitness Memory: A Critical Review." *Psychological Bulletin* 112 (1992) 284–309.
Coakley, J. F. "The Anointing at Bethany and the Priority of John." *JBL* 107 (1988) 241–56.
Collins, John J. *The Scepter and the Star: The Messiahs of the Dead Sea Scrolls and Other Ancient Literature*. New York: Doubleday, 1995.
Comfort, Philip W., and David P. Barrett, editors. *The Complete Text of the Earliest New Testament Manuscripts*. Grand Rapids: Baker, 1999.
Conway, Martin A. et al. "The Formation of Flashbulb Memories." *Memory and Cognition* 22 (1994) 326–43.
Coogan, Michael D. et al., editors. "Chronological Table of Rulers." In *The New Oxford Annotated Bible*, 530 ES–533 ES. 3rd ed. Oxford: Oxford University Press, 2001.
Corley, Kathleen E. "Feminist Myths of Christian Origins." In *Reimagining Christian Origins: A Colloquium Honoring Burton L. Mack*, edited by Elizabeth A. Castelli and Hal Taussig, 51–67. Valley Forge, PA: Trinity, 1996.
———. "Salome and Jesus at Table in the *Gospel of Thomas*." *Semeia* 86 (1999) 85–97.
Crossan, John Dominic. *The Birth of Christianity: Discovering What Happened in the Years Immediately after the Execution of Jesus*. San Francisco: HarperSanFrancisco, 1998.
———. *The Historical Jesus: The Life of a Mediterranean Jewish Peasant*. San Francisco: HarperSanFrancisco, 1991.
———. "Mark and the Relatives of Jesus." *NovT* 15 (1973) 82–113.
———. *Who Killed Jesus?: Exposing the Roots of Anti-Semitism in the Gospel Story of the Death of Jesus*. San Francisco: HarperSanFrancisco, 1995.
Crossan, John Dominic, and Johnathan L. Reed. *Excavating Jesus: Beneath the Stones, Behind the Texts*. San Francisco: HarperSanFrancisco, 2001.
Crossley, James G. *The Date of Mark's Gospel: Insight from the Law in Earliest Christianity*. JSNTSup 266. London: T & T Clark, 2004.
Cullmann, O., and A. J. B. Higgins, translators. "The Protevangelium of James." In *New Testament Apocrypha*. Vol. 1. *Gospels and Related Writings*. Edited by Wilhelm Schneemelcher. Translated by R. McL. Wilson, 374–88. Philadelphia: Westminster, 1963.
Culpepper, R. Alan. *John, the Son of Zebedee: The Life of a Legend*. Columbia, SC: University of South Carolina Press, 1994.
D'Angelo, Mary Rose. "Reconstructing 'Real' Women in Gospel Literature: The Case of Mary Magdalene." In *Women and Christian Origins*, edited by Ross S. Kraemer and Mary Rose D'Angelo, 105–28. New York: Oxford University Press, 1999.

———. "(Re)Presentations of Women in the Gospels: John and Mark." In *Women and Christian Origins*, edited by Ross S. Kraemer and Mary Rose D'Angelo, 129–49. New York: Oxford University Press, 1999.

D'Argembeau, Arnaud, and Martial Van der Linden. "Remembering Pride and Shame: Self-Enhancement and the Phenomenology of Autobiographical Memory." *Memory* 16 (2008) 538–47.

Dart, John. *Decoding Mark*. Harrisburg, PA: Trinity, 2003.

Derrett, J. Duncan M. "Spirit-Possession and the Gerasene Demoniac." *Man*, n.s., 14 (1979) 286–93.

———. "Why Jesus Blessed the Children (Mk 10:13–16 par.)." *NovT* 25 (1983) 1–18.

Dewey, Joanna. "Mark as Interwoven Tapestry: Forecasts and Echoes for a Listening Audience." *CBQ* 53 (1991) 221–36.

———. "Oral Methods of Structuring Narrative in Mark." *Interpretation* 43 (1989) 32–44.

———. "The Survival of Mark's Gospel: A Good Story?" *JBL* 123 (2004) 495–507.

Dijkhuizen, P. "An Investigation into the Historical, Hermeneutical, and Gospel-Critical Parameters for the Interpretation of the Symbol of Resurrection." MTh Thesis, University of South Africa, 1997.

Dunbabin, Katherine M. D. "Ut Greaco More Biberetur: Greeks and Romans on the Dining Couch." In *Meals in a Social Context: Aspects of the Communal Meal in the Hellenistic and Roman World*, edited by Inge Nielsen and Hanne S. Nielsen, 81–101. Aarhus Studies in Mediterranean Antiquity 1. Aarhus, Denmark: Aarhus University Press, 1998.

Edwards, Derek, and David Middleton. "Joint Remembering: Constructing an Account of Shared Experience through Conversational Discourse." *Discourse Processes* 9 (1986) 423–59.

Edwards, Douglas R. "Khirbet Qana: From Jewish Village to Christian Pilgrim Site." In *The Roman and Byzantine Near East*. Vol. 3, edited by J. H. Humphrey, 101–32. JRASup 49. Portsmouth, RI: Journal of Roman Archaeology, 2002.

Ehrman, Bart D. *Lost Christianities: The Battles for Scripture and the Faiths We Never Knew*. Oxford: Oxford University Press, 2003.

———. *Lost Scriptures: Books that Did Not Make It into the New Testament*. Oxford: Oxford University Press, 2003.

———. *Peter, Paul, and Mary Magdalene: The Followers of Jesus in History and Legend*. Oxford: Oxford University Press, 2006.

Eisenman, Robert H. *James the Brother of Jesus*. New York: Viking, 1997.

Eldershaw, Lynn P. "Collective Identity and the Postcharismatic Fate of Shambhala International." *Novo Religio: The Journal of Alternative and Emergent Religions* 10, 4 (2007) 72–102.

Elliott, John H. *1 Peter: A New Translation with Introduction and Commentary*. AB 37B. New York: Doubleday, 2000.

———. *A Home for the Homeless: A Sociological Exegesis of 1 Peter, Its Situation and Strategy*. Philadelphia: Fortress, 1981.

———. "The Roman Provenance of 1 Peter and the Gospel of Mark: A Response to David Dungan." In *Colloquy on New Testament Studies*, edited by Bruce C. Corley, 181–94. Macon, GA: Mercer University Press, 1983.

Epiphanius. *The Panarion of St. Epiphanius, Bishop of Salamis: Selected Passages*. Translated by Philip R. Amidon. New York: Oxford University Press, 1990.

Eshel, Hanan. *The Dead Sea Scrolls and the Hasmonean State*. Grand Rapids: Eerdmans, 2008.
Eusebius. *The History of the Church*. Translated by G. A. Williamson. London: Penguin, 1965.
Feldmeier, R. "Excursus: The Portrayal of Peter in the Synoptic Gospels." In Martin Hengel, *Studies in the Gospel of Mark*, 59–63, 161–62. Philadelphia: Fortress, 1985.
Finegan, Jack. *Handbook of Biblical Chronology: Principles of Time Reckoning in the Ancient World and Problems of Chronology in the Bible*. Princeton: Princeton University Press, 1964.
Flusser, David. "'The House of David' on an Ossuary." *Israel Museum Journal* 5 (1986) 37–40.
———. *Judaism and the Origins of Christianity*. Jerusalem: Magnes Press, 1988.
Fredriksen, Paula. *Jesus of Nazareth King of the Jews: A Jewish Life and the Emergence of Christianity*. New York: Knopf, 1999.
Freedman, H. *Pesaḥim*. Vol. 4 of *The Babylonian Talmud*. Isidore Epstein, general editor. London: Soncino Press, 1983.
Freyne, Sean. *Galilee From Alexander the Great to Hadrian 323 BCE to 135 CE: A Study of Second Temple Judaism*. Wilmington, DE: M. Glazier, 1980.
Gerhardsson, B. "Mark and the Female Witnesses." In *Dumu-e2-dub-ba-a: Studies in Honor of Åke W. Sjoberg*, edited by Hermann Behrens et al., 219–22. Philadelphia: University Museum, 1989.
Giacosa, Ilaria G. *A Taste of Ancient Rome*. Translated by Mary Taylor Simeti. Chicago: University of Chicago Press, 1992.
Gibson, Shimon. *The Final Days of Jesus: The Archaeological Evidence*. New York: HarperCollins, 2009.
Goldstein, Jonathan A. *I Maccabees: A New Translation with Introduction and Commentary*. AB 41. Garden City, NY: Doubleday, 1976.
———. *II Maccabees: A New Translation with Introduction and Commentary*. AB 41A. Garden City, NY: Doubleday, 1983.
Gordon, Matthew S. *The Rise of Islam*. Westport, CT: Greenwood Press, 2005.
Gorenberg, G. *The End of Days: Fundamentalism and the Struggle for the Temple Mount*. New York: Free Press, 2000.
Grantham-McGregor, S. M., and C. C. Ani. "Undernutrition and Mental Development." In *Nutrition and Brain*, edited by J. D. Fernstrom et al., 1–18. Nestle Nutrition Workshop Series Clinical & Performance Program 5. Basel: Karger, 2001.
Grassi, Joseph A. *The Secret Identity of the Beloved Disciple*. New York: Paulist, 1992.
Hachlili, Rachel. "The Goliath Family of Jericho: Funerary Inscriptions from a First Century A.D. Jewish Monumental Tomb." *BASOR* 235 (1979) 31–66.
———. "Hebrew Names, Personal Names, Family Names and Nicknames of Jews in the Second Temple Period." In *Families and Family Relations*, edited by Jan W. Van Henten and Athalya Brenner, 83–115. STAR 2. Leiden: Deo, 2000.
———. *Jewish Funerary Customs, Practices, and Rites in the Second Temple Period*. Leiden: Brill, 2005.
———. "Names and Nicknames of the Jews in Second Temple Times." *ErIsr* 17 (1984) 188–211 (English summary on 9–10).
Haines-Eitzen, Kim. *Guardians of Letters: Literacy, Power, and the Transmitters of Early Christian Literature*. Oxford: Oxford University Press, 2000.

Hanson, K. C. "All in the Family: Kinship in Agrarian Roman Palestine." In *The Social World of the New Testament: Insights and Models,* edited by Jerome H. Neyrey and Eric C. Steward, 25–46. Peabody, MA: Hendrickson, 2008.

———. "BTB Readers Guide: Kinship." *BTB* 24 (1994) 183–94.

———. "The Herodians and Mediterranean Kinship. Part I: Genealogy and Descent." *BTB* 19 (1989) 75–84.

———. "The Herodians and Mediterranean Kinship. Part II: Marriage and Divorce." *BTB* 19 (1989) 142–51.

Hanson, K. C., and Douglas E. Oakman. *Palestine in the Time of Jesus: Social Structures and Social Conflicts.* Minneapolis: Fortress, 1998.

Harrington, Daniel J. *The Maccabean Revolt: Anatomy of a Biblical Revolution.* Wilmington, DE: M. Glazier, 1988.

Haslehurst, R. S. T. "Mark, My Son." *Theology* 13 (1926) 34–36.

Havelock, Eric A. *Preface to Plato.* Cambridge: Belknap, 1963.

Hengel, Martin. *Acts and the History of Earliest Christianity.* Translated by John Bowden. Philadelphia: Fortress, 1980.

———. *The "Hellenization" of Judaea in the First Century after Christ.* Philadelphia: Trinity, 1989.

———. *The Johannine Question.* Philadelphia: Fortress, 1989.

———. *Studies in the Gospel of Mark.* Translated by John Bowden. Philadelphia: Fortress, 1985.

Henige, David. *Oral Historiography.* New York: Longman, 1982.

Herford, R. T. *Christianity in Talmud and Midrash.* London: Williams & Norgate, 1903. Reprinted in New York by KTAV, 1975.

Hesse, B., and P. Wapnish. "Can Pig Remains be Used for Ethnic Diagnosis in the Ancient Near East?" In *The Archaeology of Israel: Constructing the Past, Interpreting the Present,* edited by N. A. Silberman and D. B. Small, 238–70. Sheffield: Sheffield Academic, 1997.

Higham, T. M. "The Experimental Study of the Transmission of Rumour." *British Journal of Psychology* 42 (1951) 42–55.

Hoehner, H. W. "The Date of the Death of Herod the Great." In *Chronos, Kairos, Christos: Nativity and Chronological Studies Presented to Jack Finegan,* edited by Jerry Vardaman and Edwin M. Yamauchi, 101–11. Winona Lake, IN: Eisenbrauns, 1989.

Horsley, Richard. A. *Galilee: History, Politics, People.* Valley Forge, PA: Trinity, 1995.

———. "High Priests and the Politics of Roman Palestine." *JSJ* 17 (1986) 23–55.

Humphrey, Colin J., and W. G. Waddington. "Astronomy and the Date of the Crucifixion." In *Chronos, Kairos, Christos: Nativity and Chronological Studies Presented to Jack Finegan,* edited by Jerry Vardaman and Edwin M. Yamauchi, 165–81. Winona Lake, IN: Eisenbrauns, 1989.

Hunzinger, C.-H., "Babylon als Deckname für Rom und die Datierung des 1. Petrusbriefes." In *Gottes Wort und Gottes Land: Hans-Wilhelm Hertzberg zum 70,* edited by Henning Graf Reventlow, 67–77. Göttingen: Vandenhoeck & Ruprecht, 1965.

Ilan, T. *Jewish Women in Greco-Roman Palestine: An Inquiry into Image and Status.* TSAJ 44. Tübingen: Mohr Siebeck, 1995.

———. *Lexicon of Jewish Names in Late Antiquity: Part I, Palestine 330 BCE–200 CE.* TSAJ 91. Tübingen: Mohr Siebeck, 2002.

Isenberg, Wesley W., translator. "The Gospel of Philip (II, 3)." In *The Nag Hammadi Library in English,* edited by James M. Robinson, 131–51. Leiden: Brill, 1977.

Jacobus, Donald L. "Confessions of a Genealogical Heretic." *The New England Historical and Genealogical Register* 112 (1958) 81–87.

———. "On the Nature of Genealogical Evidence." *The New England Historical and Genealogical Register* 92 (1938) 213–20.

Janjuha-Jivraj, Shaheena. "The Impact of the Mother during Family Business Succession: Examples from the Asian Business Community." *Journal of Ethnic and Migration Studies* 30 (2004) 781–97.

Jefford, C. N. "Mark, John." *ABD* 4:557–58.

Jeremias, Joachim. *Jerusalem in the Time of Jesus: An Investigation into Economic and Social Conditions during the New Testament Period.* Translated by F. H. and C. H. Cavel. Philadelphia: Fortress, 1969.

Jerome. *On Illustrious Men (De Viris Illustribus).* Translated by Thomas B. Halton. FC 100. Washington, DC: Catholic University of America Press, 1999.

Jobes, Karen H. *1 Peter.* Grand Rapids: Baker Academic, 2005.

Johnson, Marshall D. *The Purpose of the Biblical Genealogies with Special Reference to the Setting of the Genealogies of Jesus.* 2d ed. SNTSMS 8. Cambridge: Cambridge University Press, 1988.

Johnson, Ronald E. "The Retention of Qualitative Changes in Learning." *Journal of Verbal Learning and Verbal Behavior* 1(1962) 218–23.

Josephus. Translated by H. St. J. Thackeray et al. 10 vols. LCL. Cambridge: Harvard University Press, 1926–1965.

Kaplan, Zvi, and Norma Baumel Joseph. "Bar Mitzvah, Bat Mitzvah." *EncJud* 3:164–66.

Kauffman, M. W. *American Brutus: John Wilkes Booth and the Lincoln Conspiracies.* New York: Random House, 2004.

Kelber, Werner. *The Oral and Written Gospel.* Philadelphia: Fortress, 1983.

Kokkinos, Nikos. *The Herodian Dynasty: Origins, Role in Society and Eclipse.* JSPSup 30. Sheffield, Scheffield Academic, 1998.

Kraemer, Ross S. "Implicating Herodias and Her Daughter in the Death of John the Baptizer: A (Christian) Theological Strategy?" *JBL* 125 (2006): 321–49.

Leon, Harry J. *The Jews of Ancient Rome.* Philadelphia: Jewish Publication Society, 1960.

Levine, Lee I. *Jerusalem: Portrait of the City in the Second Temple Period 538 BCE–70 CE.* Philadelphia: Jewish Publication Society, 2002.

Malina, Bruce. J., *The New Testament World: Insights from Cultural Anthropology.* rev. ed. Louisville, KY: Westminster John Knox, 1993.

Malina, Bruce J., and Richard L. Rohrbaugh. *Social-Science Commentary on the Synoptic Gospels.* Minneapolis: Fortress, 1992.

Marcus, Joel. *Mark 1–8: A New Translation with Introduction and Commentary.* AB 27. New York: Doubleday, 2000.

Martin, R. P. "Mark, John." *ISBE* 4:259–60.

Masse, W. Bruce et al. "Waha'ula *heiau*, the regional and symbolic context of Hawai'i Island's 'Red Mouth' temple." *Asian Perspectives* 30 (1991) 19–56.

McDonnell, Myles. "Writing, Copying, and Autograph Manuscripts in Ancient Rome." *CQ* 46 (1996) 469–91.

Meade, David G. *Pseudonymity and Canon.* WUNT 39. Tübingen: Mohr Siebeck, 1986.

Meier, John P. "Antioch." In *Antioch and Rome: New Testament Cradles of Catholic Christianity*, edited by Raymond E. Brown and John P. Meier, 11–86. New York: Paulist, 1983.

———. "The Brothers and Sisters of Jesus in Ecumenical Perspective." *CBQ* 54 (1992) 1–28.

———. *A Marginal Jew: Rethinking the Historical Jesus*. Vol. 1. *The Roots of the Problem and the Person*. ABRL. New York: Doubleday, 1991.

Metzger, Bruce M. "Literary Forgeries and Canonical Pseudepigrapha." *JBL* 91 (1972) 3–24.

Meyer, Marvin, and Esther A. de Boer. *The Gosepls of Mary: The Secret Tradition of Mary Magdalene, the Companion of Jesus*. San Francisco: HarperSan Francisco, 2004.

Miller, Stuart S. *Studies in the History and Traditions of Sepphoris*. SJLA 37. Leiden: Brill, 1984.

Moxnes, Halvor. *Putting Jesus in His Place: A Radical View of Household and Kingdom*. Louisville, KY: Westminster John Knox, 2003.

Murphy-O'Connor, Jerome. "The Cenacle and Community: The Background of Acts 2:44–45." In *Scripture and Other Artifacts: Essays on the Bible and Archaeology in Honor of Philip J. King*, edited by M. D. Coogan et al., 296–310. Louisville, KY: Westminster John Knox, 1994.

———. "The Cenacle: Topographical Setting for Acts 2:44–45." In *The Book of Acts in Its Palestinian Setting*, edited by Richard Bauckham, 303–21. Vol. 4 of *The Book of Acts in Its First Century Setting*. Edited by Bruce W. Winter. Grand Rapids: Eerdmans, 1995.

———. "What Really Happened at Gesemane?" In *Jesus: The Last Day*, edited by M. D. Meinhardt, 39–58. Washington, DC: Biblical Archaeology Society, 2003.

Naveh, J. "Nameless People." *IEJ* 40 (1990) 108–23.

Neisser, Ulric. "John Dean's Memory: A Case Study." *Cognition* 9 (1981) 1–22.

Nineham, Dennis E. *Saint Mark*. Pelican Gospel Commentaries. Baltimore, MD: Penguin, 1963.

Noy, David. "The Sixth Hour is the Mealtime for Scholars: Jewish Meals in the Roman World." In *Meals in a Social Context: Aspects of the Communal Meal in the Hellenistic and Roman World*, edited by Inge Nielsen and Hanne S. Nielsen, 134–44. Aarhus Studies in Mediterranean Antiquity 1. Aarhus, Denmark: Aarhus University Press, 1998.

Oakman, Douglas E. "Was Jesus a Peasant?: Implications for Reading the Jesus Tradition (Luke 10:30–35)." In *The Social World of the New Testament: Insights and Models*, edited by Jerome H. Neyrey and Eric C. Stewart, 123–40. Peabody, MA: Hendrickson, 2008.

Painter, John. *Just James: The Brother of Jesus in History and Tradition*. 2d ed. Columbia, SC: University of South Carolina Press, 1997.

Parker, Pierson. "John the Son of Zebedee and the Fourth Gospel." *JBL* 81 (1962) 35–43.

Piggott, Stuart. "The Sources of Geoffrey of Monmouth I. The 'Pre-Roman' King-List." *Antiquity* 15 (1941) 269–86.

Pliny the Younger. *Letters and Panegyricus*. Vol. 2. Translated by Betty Radice. LCL 59. Cambridge: Harvard University Press, 1969.

Rahmani, L. Y. *A Catalogue of Jewish Ossuaries in the Collections of the State of Israel*. Jerusalem: The Israel Antiquities Authority/The Israel Academy of Sciences and Humanities, 1994.

Reed, Jonathan L. *Archaeology and the Galilean Jesus: A Re-examination of the Evidence*. Harrisburg, PA: Trinity, 2000.

Richards, Ernest R. *Paul and First-Century Letter Writing: Secretaries, Composition, and Collection*. Downers Grove, IL: Intervarsity, 2004.

Richardson, Peter. *Building Jewish in the Roman East*. JSJSup 92. Waco, TX: Baylor University Press, 2004.

Roberts, Alexander, and James Donaldson, editors. "Constitutions of the Holy Apostles." In *ANF* 7 (1951) 391–508.

Rohrbaugh, Richard L. *The New Testament in Cross-Cultural Perspective*. Matrix: The Bible in Mediterranean Context 1. Eugene, OR: Cascade, 2007.

———. "The Social Location of the Markan Audience." In *The Social World of the New Testament: Insights and Models*, edited by Jerome H. Neyrey and Eric C. Stewart, 141–62. Peabody, MA: Hendrickson, 2008.

Roller, Matthew B. *Dining Posture in Ancient Rome: Bodies, Values, and Status*. Princeton: Princeton University Press, 2006.

Rosnow, Ralph L. "Inside Rumor: A Personal Journey." *American Psychologist* 46 (1991) 484–96.

Sanders, E. P. *Judaism: Practice and Belief 63 BCE–66 CE*. London: SCM, 1992.

Sawicki, Marianne. "Magdalenes and Tiberiennes: City Women in the Entourage of Jesus." In *Transformative Encounters: Jesus and Women Re-viewed*, edited by Ingrid R. Kitzberger, 181–201. BibInt 43. Leiden: Brill, 2000.

Schauss, H. *The Jewish Festivals: History and Observance*. New York: Schocken, 1988.

Schmidt, Stephen R. "Autobiographical Memories for the September 11th Attacks: Reconstructive Errors and Emotional Impairment of Memory." *Memory and Cognition* 32 (2004) 443–54.

Schmolck, H. et al. "Memory Distortions Develop over Time: Recollections of the O. J. Simpson Trial Verdict after 15 and 32 Months." *Psychological Science* 11 (2000) 39–45.

Schnackenburg, Rudolf. *The Gospel according to St John*. Vol. 1. Translated by Kevin Smyth. New York: Seabury Press, 1980. Originally published by Herder and Herder, 1968.

Schottroff, Luise. "Women as Followers of Jesus in New Testament Times: An Exercise in Social-Historical Exegesis of the Bible." In *The Bible and Liberation, Political and Social Hermeneutics*, edited by Norman K. Gottwald, 418–27. Maryknoll, NY: Orbis, 1983.

Schüssler Fiorenza, E. *In Memory of Her: A Feminist Theological Reconstruction of Christian Origins*. New York: Crossroad, 1983.

Schürer, Emil. *The History of the Jewish People in the Age of Jesus Christ*. Vol. 1. Edited by Geza Vermes et al. rev. ed. Edinburgh: T. & T. Clark, 1973.

Schwartz, Daniel R. *Agrippa I: The Last King of Judaea*. TSAJ 23. Tübingen: Mohr Siebeck, 1990.

———. "Joseph ben Illem and the Date of Herod's Death." In *Studies in the Jewish Background of Christianity*, 157–66. WUNT 60. Tübingen: Mohr Siebeck, 1992.

Schwartz, Seth. *Josephus and Judaean Politics*. Columbia Studies in the Classical Tradition 18. Leiden: Brill, 1990.

Segev, Tom. *One Palestine, Complete: Jews and Arabs under the British Mandate*. New York: Metropolitan Books, 1999.

Senior, Donald P. "1 Peter." In *1 Peter, Jude, and 2 Peter*, edited by Daniel J. Harrington, 1–158. SP 15. Collegeville, MN: Liturgical Press, 2003.

Setzer, Claudia. "Excellent Women: Female Witness to Resurrection." *JBL* 116 (1997) 259–72.

Shanks, Hershel, and Ben Witherington III. *The Brother of Jesus*. New York: HarperCollins, 2003.

Shields, S. I. "The Latter Day Saint Movement: A Study in Survival." In *When Prophets Die: The Postcharismatic Fate of New Religious Movements*, edited by Timothy Miller, 59–78. SUNY Series on Religious Studies. Albany: State University of New York Press, 1991.

Shoemaker, Stephen J. "Rethinking the 'Gnostic Mary': Mary of Nazareth and Mary of Magdala in Early Christian Tradition." *JECS* 9 (2001) 555–95.

Sivertsen, Barbara J. "New Testament Genealogies and the Families of Mary and Joseph." *BTB* 35, 2 (2005) 43–50.

———. *The Parting of the Sea: How Volcanoes, Earthquakes, and Plagues Shaped the Story of Exodus*. Princeton: Princeton University Press, 2009.

Slingerland, H. Dixon. *Claudian Policymaking and the Early Imperial Repression of Judaism at Rome*. University of South Florida Studies in the History of Judaism 160. Atlanta: Scholars Press, 1997.

———. "Suetonius *Claudius 25.4* and the Account in Cassius Dio." *JQR* 79 (1989) 305–22.

Smallwood, E. Mary. "High Priests and Politics in Roman Palestine." *JTS*, n.s., 13 (1962) 14–34.

Smith, Dennis E. *From Symposium to Eucharist: The Banquet in the Early Christian World*. Minneapolis: Fortress, 2003.

Staniforth, M., translator. *Early Christian Writings: The Apostolic Fathers*. Harmondsworth, UK: Penguin, 1968.

Stanton, Graham N. "The Fourfold Gospel." *NTS* 43 (1997) 317–46.

Stern, Menahem. "Aspects of Jewish Society: The Priesthood and Other Classes." In *The Jewish People in the First Century*, edited by S. Safrai and M. Stern, 561–630. Philadelphia: Fortress, 1976.

———. "The Reign of Herod and the Herodian Dynasty." In *The Jewish People in the First Century*, edited by S. Safrai and M. Stern, 216–307. Philadelphia: Fortress, 1974.

———. "The Relations between Judea and Rome during the Rule of John Hyrcanus." *Zion* 26 (1961) 1–22 (in Hebrew).

Stoch M. B., and P. M. Smythe. "Undernutrition during Infancy, and Subsequent Brain Growth and Intellectual Development." In *Malnutrition, Learning, and Behavior*, edited by N. S. Scrimshaw and J. E. Gordon, 278–89. Cambridge: MIT Press, 1968.

Strange, W. A. *The Problem of the Text of Acts*. SNTSMS 71. Cambridge: Cambridge University Press, 1992.

Stephenson, Geoffrey M. et al. "An Experimental Study of Social Performance and Delay on the Testimonial Validity of Story Recall." *European Journal of Social Psychology* 13 (1983) 175–91.

Suetonius. "Lives of the Caesars: Claudius." In *Suetonius*. Vol. 2. Translated by J. C. Rolfe. LCL. Cambridge: Harvard University Press, 1997.

Swete, Henry B. *The Apocalypse of St. John: The Greek Text with Introduction, Notes, and Indices*. London: Macmillan, 1906.

———. "The Disciple Whom Jesus Loved." *JTS* 17 (1916) 371–74.

———. *The Gospel According to St. Mark: The Greek Text with Introduction, Notes, and Indices*. London: Macmillan, 1909.

Tacitus. *The Histories and the Annals*. Translated by C. H. Moore and J. Jackson. 4 vols. LCL. Cambridge: Harvard University Press, 1937.

Taylor, Joan E. "Where was Gethsemane?" In *Jesus: The Last Day*, edited by M. D. Meinhardt, 23–38. Washington, DC: Biblical Archaeology Society, 2003.
Taylor, N. H. "Palestinian Christianity and the Caligula Crisis. Part I: Social and Historical Reconstruction." *JSNT* 61 (1996) 101–24.
———. "Palestinian Christianity and the Caligula Crisis. Part II: The Markan Eschatological Discourse." *JSNT* 62 (1996) 13–41.
———. "Popular Opposition to Caligula in Jewish Palestine." *JSJ* 32 (2001) 54–70.
Theissen, Gerd. *The Gospels in Context: Social and Political History in the Synoptic Tradition.* Translated by Linda M. Maloney. Minneapolis: Fortress, 1991.
Umoh, Camillus. *The Plot to Kill Jesus: A Contextual Study of John 11:47–53*. European University Studies Series 22: Theology 696. Frankfurt am Main, Germany: Peter Lang, 2000.
VanderKam, James C. *From Joshua to Caiaphas: High Priests after the Exile*. Minneapolis: Fortress, 2004.
Vansina, Jan. *Oral Tradition as History*. Madison, WI: University of Wisconsin Press, 1985.
Vermes, Geza. *The Changing Faces of Jesus*. New York: Viking, 2000.
———. *The Complete Dead Sea Scrolls in English*. New York: Penguin, 1997.
———. *The Passion*. London: Penguin, 2006.
Waetjen, Herman C. *The Gospel of the Beloved Disciple: A Work in Two Editions*. New York: T & T Clark, 2005.
Wagenaar, Willem A. "My Memory: A Study of Autobiographical Memory over Six Years." *Cognitive Psychology* 18 (1986) 225–52.
Wahlde, Urban C. von. "Archaeology and John's Gospel." In *Jesus and Archaeology*, edited by James. H. Charlesworth, 523–86. Grand Rapids: Eerdmans, 2006.
Wallace, Anthony F. C. "Revitalization Movements." *American Anthropologist* 58 (1956) 264–81.
Wallraff, M., editor. *Julius Africanus Chronographiae: The Extant Fragments*. Translated by William Adler. Berlin: de Gruyter, 2007.
Ward, Seth. "Sepphoris in Sacred Geography." In *Galilee through the Centuries*, edited by Eric M. Meyers, 391–406. Winona Lake, IN: Eisenbrauns, 1999.
Wegner, Judith R. *Chattel or Person?: The Status of Women in the Mishnah*. New York: Oxford University Press, 1988.
Weeden, Theodore J. *Mark: Traditions in Conflict*. Philadelphia: Fortress, 1971.
Wiarda, Timothy. "Peter as Peter in the Gospel of Mark." *NTS* 45 (1999) 19–37.
Williams, Margaret H. "Palestinian Jewish Personal Names in Acts." In *The Book of Acts in Its Palestinian Setting*, edited by Richard Bauckham 79–113. Vol. 4 of *The Book of Acts in Its First Century Setting*. Edited by Bruce W. Winter. Grand Rapids: Eerdmans, 1995.
Wilson, Ian. *Murder at Golgotha: Revisiting the Most Famous Crime Scene in History*. New York: St. Martin's, 2005.
Wilson, Robert R. *Genealogy and History in the Biblical World*. New Haven: Yale University Press, 1977.
Wise, Michael O. *The First Messiah: Investigating the Savior before Christ*. San Francisco: HarperSanFrancisco, 1999.
Wise, Michael O., and James D. Tabor. "The Messiah at Qumran." *BAR* 18, 6 (1992) 60–65.

Witherington, Ben III, *Women in the Ministry of Jesus: A Study of Jesus' Attitudes to Women and Their Role as Reflected in His Earthly Life*. SNTSMS 51. Cambridge: Cambridge University Press, 1984.

Yadin, Yigael. *Bar-Kokhba: The Rediscovery of the Legendary Hero of the Second Jewish Revolt against Rome*. New York: Random House, 1971.

———. *Masada: Herod's Fortress and the Zealots' Last Stand*. Translated by Moshe Pearlman. Jerusalem: Steimatzky, 1988.

www.ingramcontent.com/pod-product-compliance
Lightning Source LLC
Chambersburg PA
CBHW072204160426
43197CB00012B/2513